AF265844

Devour
Art & Lit Canada

Devour:
Art & Lit Canada

is dedicated to the Canadian voice.

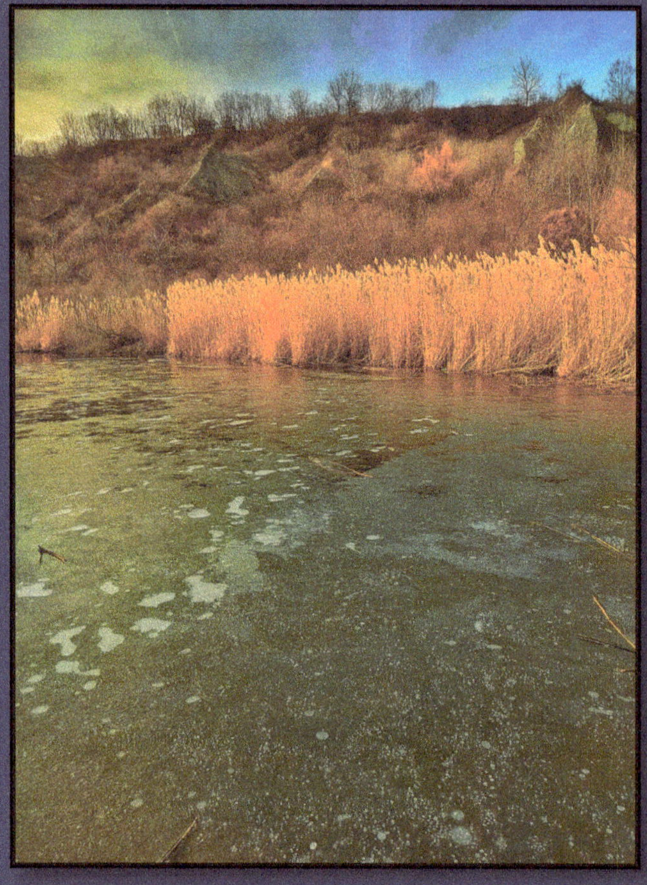

Richard M. Grove

978-1-989786-90-1 – Soft Cover

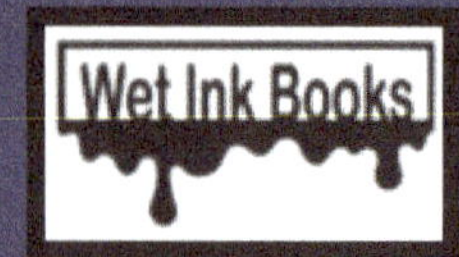

www.WetInkBooks.com

ISSN 2561-1321
Issue 016

Devour

Art & Lit Canada

Find some of Canada's
finest authors, photographers and artists
featured in every issue.

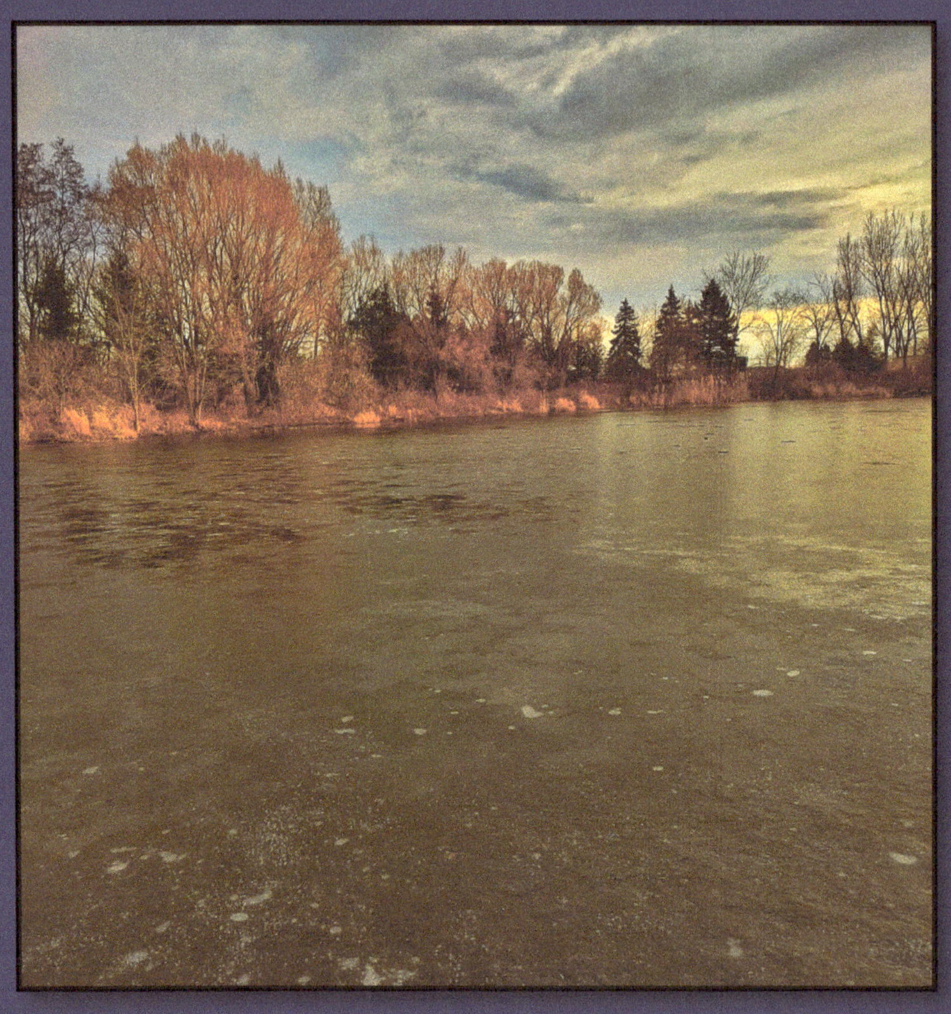

Richard M. Grove

The mission of *Devour:*
Art and Lit Canada

is to promote Canadian culture by
bringing world-wide readers some of the best
Canadian literature, art and photography.

Devour: Art and Lit Canada
ISSN 2561-1321
Special Issue 016
Spring 2023

5 Greystone Walk Drive
Unit 408
Toronto, Ontario, Canada, M1K 5J5
DevourArtAndLitCanada@gmail.com

Feature Photography – Olaf Dijkstra

Editor-in-Chief – Richard M. Grove
Layout and Design – Richard M. Grove
Front and Back Cover – Richard M. Grove

Welcome to this 16th issue of Devour: Art & Lit Canada.

As usual we are bringing you some of Canada's most talented writers, poets and photographers.

This special issue is primarily dedicated to the winners of the 2021 and 2022 Don Gutteridge Poetry Award. Congratulations to all of the winners.

Something fun and interesting are the Sunset Over Walmart poems. You will find an explanation for those poems with an intro on page 118.

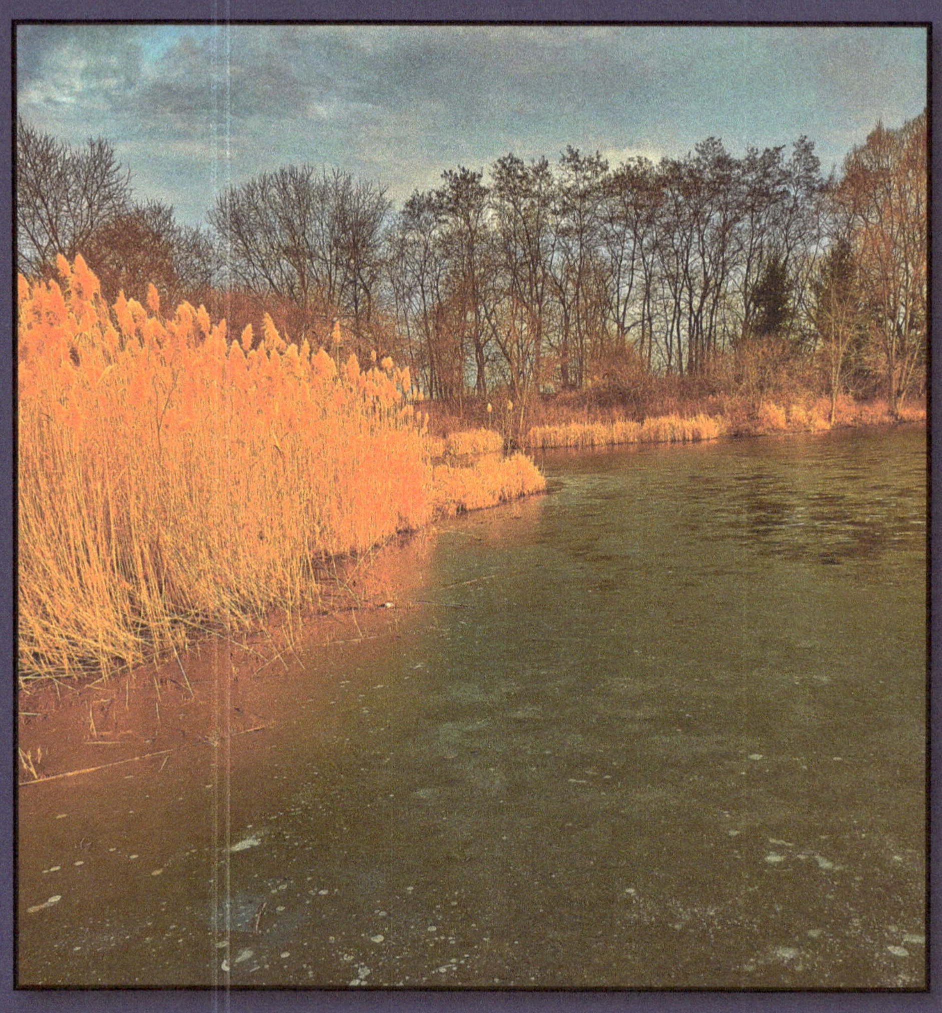

Richard M. Grove

Devour
Art & Lit Canada

Content

Thank you **Olaf Dijkstra** for your wonderful photographs. Olaf has retiring from being the Photography Curator for the "Canada Coast to Coast to Coast" section. He has moved back to the Netherlands – Canada's loss is the Netherlands gain. Keep an eye open for more of his photographs in future issues.

We will announce the new Photography Curator of the Canada Coast to Coast to Coast section in the coming Summer issue.

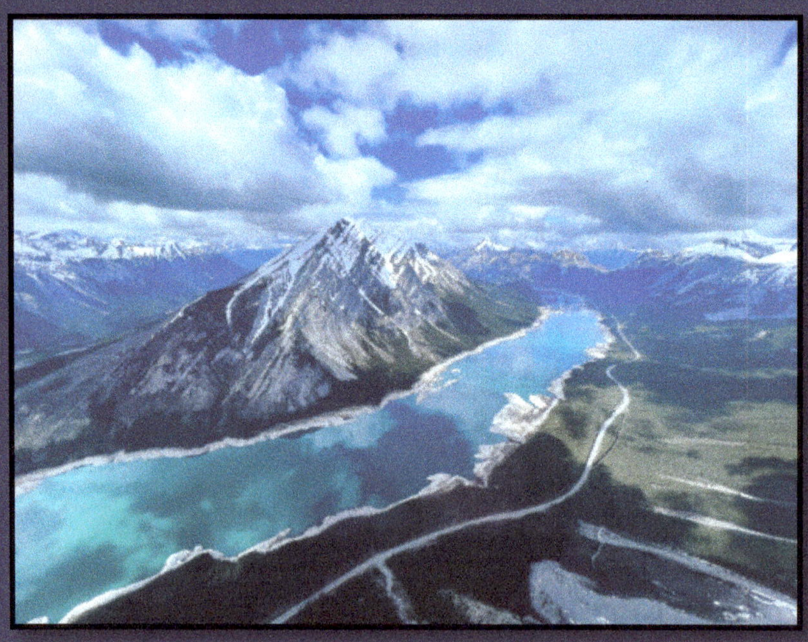

Spray Lakes in Canmore
Olaf Dijkstra

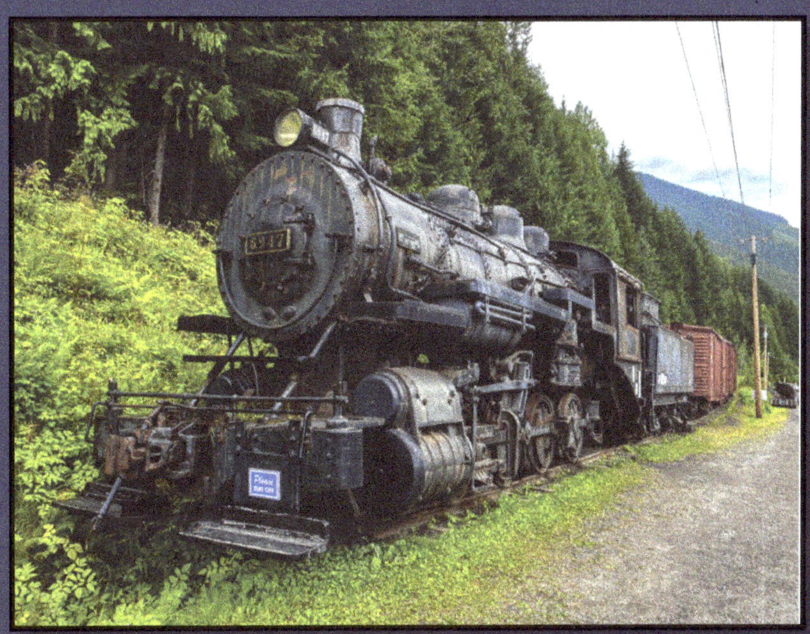

Old loc in Sandon
Olaf Dijkstra

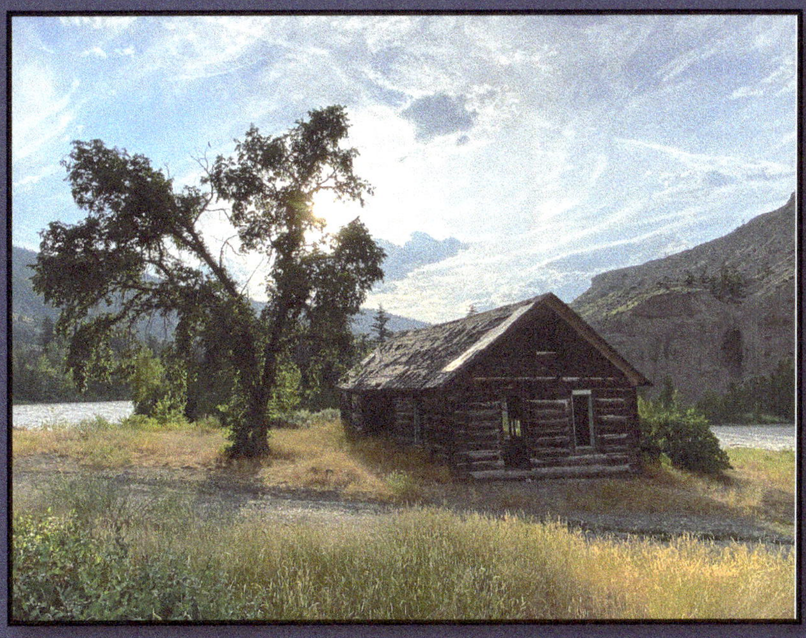

Pothole Ranch in Farwell Canyon
Olaf Dijkstra

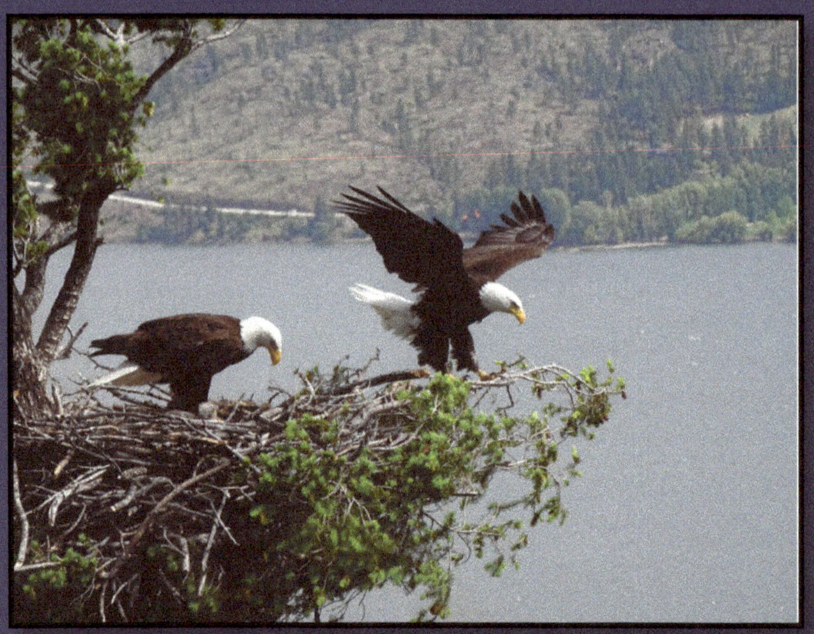

Eagle parents on nest
Olaf Dijkstra

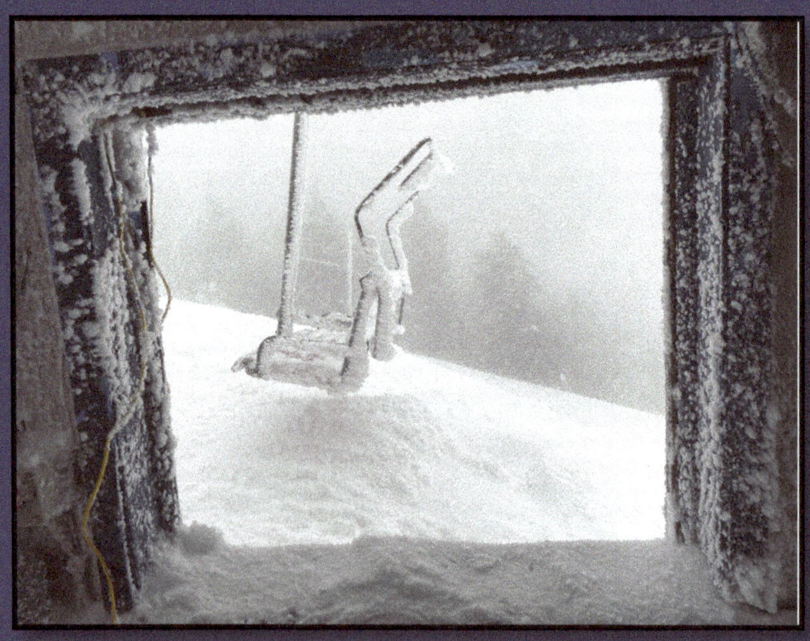

Abandoned chairlift on Crystal Mountain
Olaf Dijkstra

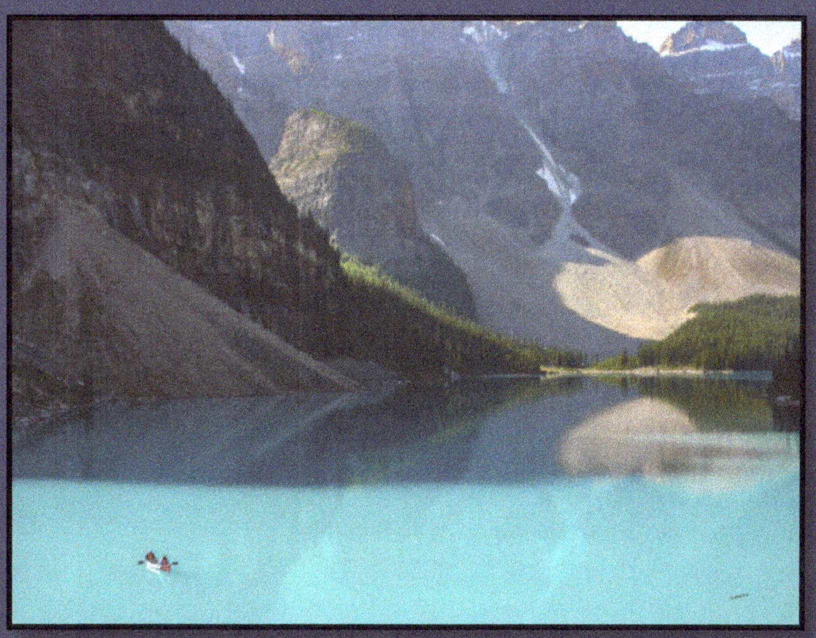

Canoe on Moraine Lake
Olaf Dijkstra

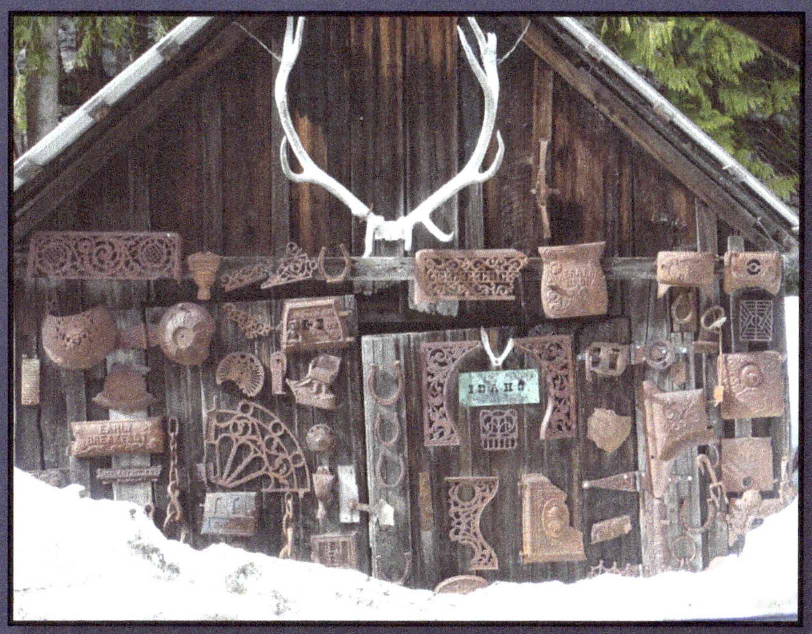

Decorated cabin in ghost town of Cody, BC
Olaf Dijkstra

2022 Don Gutteridge Poetry Award
1st Prize

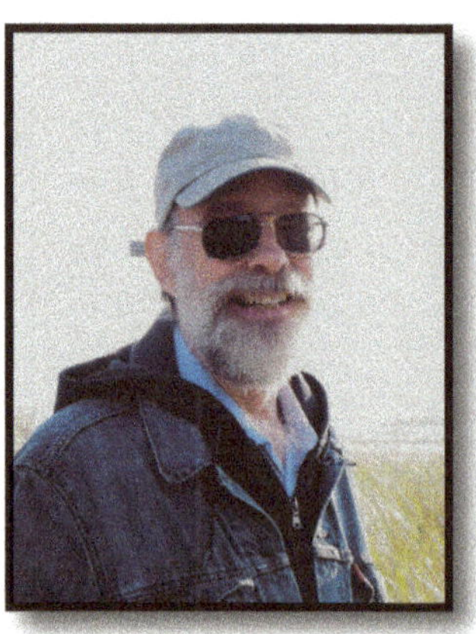

Title: ***Mangoes from the Seventh Dimension***

Author: **John Tyndall**

ISBN: **978-1-989786-84-0**

Publisher: **Wet Ink Books**

Purchase copies at — www.WetInkBooks.com
or Amazon.ca or Amazon.com

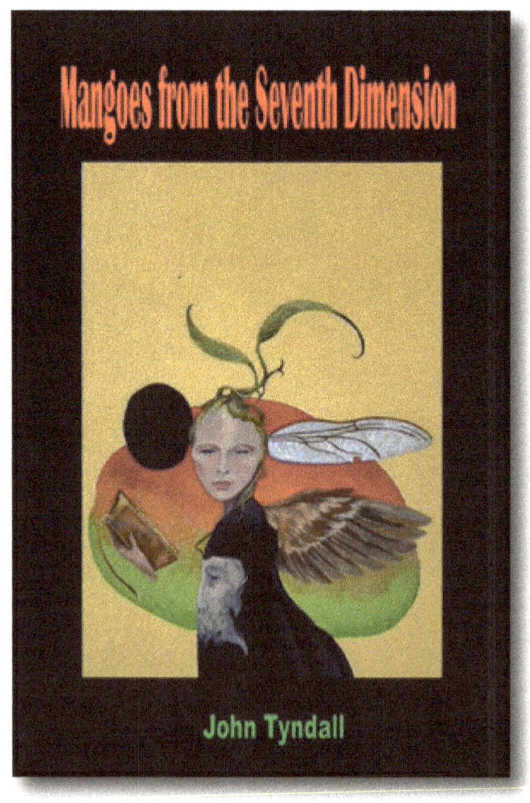

Flinders' Fingers

Flinders Petrie
on Egyptian expedition
methodically dug
down through layers
of potsherds, layers
of remote time
detailed the fragments
recorded their location
devised a classification
of successive cultures
and even where no
vessels remained *in situ*
sometimes the contents
somehow still lingered
with sand much darker
at one ancient level
where his fingers
the first in millennia
and in the name of Her
Majesty, Queen Victoria
grasped and released
fragrant sacred perfume
for the Scorpion god

A Tom's Caution

Don't you ever dare call me
your sweet chocolate chip cat
I don't care what you dreamt
what a non-existent review
of a non-existent book
in a non-existent mag
said was your best line yet
because if I want a real poem
about a real son-of-a-mog
I'll head back overseas
to the land of poets I remember
from the red adventures
of all my sires before me
to hell with your *nine lives*
scads of dads in the past
we knew this author, Hugh
I think was his name
and although Esther, the poem's
woman was a fiction
that guy could really write
about torn ears, sharp teeth
the fights and the screams
so I don't give a flying finch
about all the exotic tomcats
who loll about you all day
and you'd better believe
I could sail to Blighty
aboard any ship I choose
and when I got there
I wouldn't languish
on a gravesite like some dog

I'd be catching and killing
hot and kicking rabbits
because while you apes
were struggling to quit
the homey, leafy canopy
my ancestors were kings
of the desert night
and surviving on blood
without a drop of water
thus, my precious monkey
take heed, for if you ever
call *me* your chocolate chip cat
I'll scratch your eyes out

Danu

I come to her river
on a spring morning
mist rising, robin returning
when I hear the splash
of her horse's hoofs
'tis Danu, queen
of the Celtic gods
of the green isle
she bends to caress
my cheek, saying
Come here
I thee encharm
and when she departs
an elflock, twisted
in my beard, remains

I come to her river
at midsummer noon
cloud floating, finch circling
in the blue heavens
and from atop her steed
Danu, the mother of all
leans to caress my cheek
my head, saying
Come here
I thee encharm
Come to me
I thee enchant
and when she rides off
elflocks, twisted in my beard
in my hair, remain

I come to her river
on an autumn evening
rain falling, blackbird leaving
Danu, the great goddess

dismounts at the river-bank
stretches to caress my cheek
my head, my spine, saying
Come here
I thee encharm
Come to me
I thee enchant
Come at my call
I thee ensorcell
and when she remounts
and disappears upriver
elflocks, twisted in my beard
in my hair, down my back, remain

I come to her river
at midnight mid-winter
ice cracking, crow sleeping
under the silver stars
Danu, mistress of changes
strides towards me
reaches to caress my cheek
my head, my spine
my waist, saying
Come here
I thee encharm
Come to me
I thee enchant
Come at my call
I thee ensorcell
Come with me now away
I thee enthrall
and when she claims
her stallion charger
elflocks, twisted in my muzzle
my forelock, my mane
my tail, remain
forevermore

Pollen Angels

*If she could escape, she thought, just for a moment, out
of her personal mind into their communally single one, she
would know at last what it was like to be an angel.*
David Malouf, Remembering Babylon

Out of hexagonal cells
sexless sisters fly forth
to ensure the ripened
fruit of the tree
which is in the midst
of the garden, yea
even of the tree of life

Without these squadrons
of soldiering workers
you would look unto a land
flowing with neither
milk nor honey

To you, mirror image
of the Hiver of heaven
flights of pollen angels
wing their way, how many
may dance upon you

Be not afraid
of their sacred sound
their flaming sword
east of the sunrise

Be still

Let them swarm

Thou

for whom three identical
snowflakes alight upon
an upturned face

for whom imaginal dragonflies
wrinkle-winged and damp
emerge into the air

for whom waterfall run-off
roars over rock
in foam crescendo

for whom glaciers
roll granite debris
with abandon

for whom ancient ice
releases ancient oxygen
to ring a drinking-glass

for whom the grape
gives up nectar
and a beautiful stain

for whom Grass Pink
Rose Pogonia and Calypso
orchids lure eye-glance

for whom tears well up
and slip down
from sorrow and joy

for whom the heart drum
beats the rhythm
of all dance

To Keep Now Still

Working title of William Golding's *The Scorpion God*

The boy-king is dead
from fracture and malaria
long dead the kings of Egypt
all their gold and alabaster
will not call them forth
again to the Black Land
their chipped, eyeless statues
feign eternity, a still
point that never exists
outside a starry life
wheeling, flowing, burning
leaving Great House behind
on display in glass cases
we create to keep *now* forever
when every Pharaoh, everyone
will become as mummy dust
and even the pyramids
over time will be levelled
and gone

Tutankhamun's Mask

The mask that encased the boy-king's face
looms before my face in its museum case
as I dare to imagine wearing the relic
the mask of the golden breath of dawn
carnelian and turquoise coming forth by day
azure stone the sky at Nilotic twilight
can anyone hear me through burnished gold
my lips desert dry, papyrus dry my skin
my arms cross with the crook and the flail
although I have not conspired with demons
the cobra and the vulture upon my brow
fail to protect me from the kiss of chaos
my blessèd brain through the nostrils gone
lungs, liver, intestines, stomach reside in jars
priests remove, erect, replace the royal member
sacred salts of natron infuse the earthly body
the ka strains beneath linen, gold, wood, stone
to recognize the visage of father the sun
but sees only a reflection in the tempered glass
my eyes overlaying the empty gaze of Pharaoh

2022 Don Gutteridge Poetry Award
2nd Prize

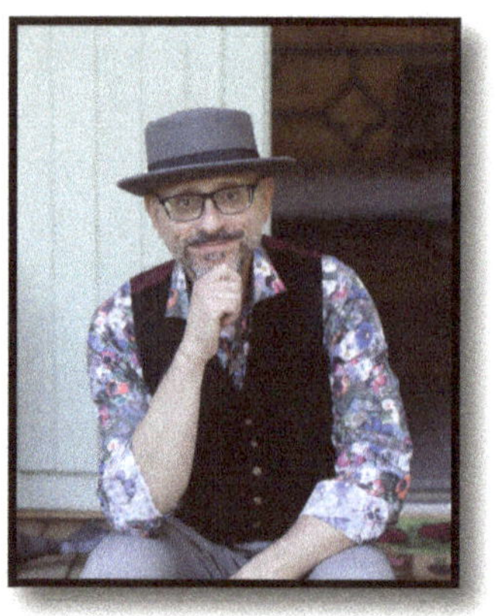

Title: *Wait, What?*

Author: **Richard-Yves Sitoski**

ISBN: **978-1-989786-83-3**

Publisher: **Wet Ink Books**

Purchase copies at — www.WetInkBooks.com
or Amazon.ca or Amazon.com

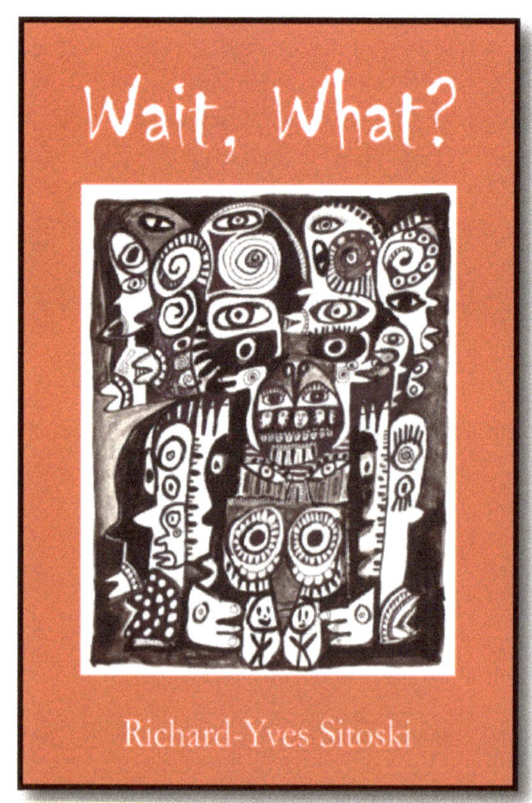

Conception

Does it not make sense that I remember
the moment of conception? I was there.

Did I not start off as a slurry,
the grey-green of skies before a tornado—

one that tears the roof off
without disturbing the china?

Escape

Mother drags me by the collar into playgrounds
but I escape. I'm hidden, like writing

on a face-down sheet of paper.
What?

Haven't you kids ever seen
a boy who fears erasers?

God

I draw a space shuttle bound
for the station where God lives.

God's been in orbit so long
he's lost all bone mass.

Look at him, floating there.
So small I could put him in a jar.

Father

Ignore him?
Tonight he's being a glove

lined with fish hooks.

Uniform

A name tag, an apron,
a polyester polo, black pants,

and customers who add
"just a" before your title.

Work

On a good day
work can be enjoyed

like eating alone
in a restaurant

when stood up
on a date.

Essential

As in most jobs
I feel necessary but ignored,

like the text
on a fire extinguisher.

Dismissal

By the time I got fired I was Ouroboros
who had reached the end of his long body

and had flipped himself inside out.
I didn't believe the hawk

circling the parking lot, who reassured me
I was no more damaged by my job

than numbers are by arithmetic.

Valentine

I meant it when I said
that in a firing squad

one guy is issued blanks,
and if she found herself

against the wall,
I hoped that guy was me.

Uh-oh

Of course I'm upset. There's a radio on
in the next apartment, and I can't stand it

because I know what the announcer will say
before he thinks it.

Bipolar

I ask myself how I can power a lightbulb
with my bare hands

yet still remain curious
about the taste of nightshade berries.

Relief

Smashing things is a matter of life and death.
Relief is trapped inside and suffocating.

Sometimes I'm not even mad.
I just break plates like Greeks at a wedding

when they set free arguments
resolved in advance.

Morning

This morning an Irish setter barked at me
and I'm crying again

because I'm clearly as ugly
as a strip club with the lights on.

Plans

Look! says the day. *I have plans for you!*
The day has plans for us all.

Including June bugs, who come
with orders to die on windowsills.

Allergic

She couldn't take it any longer. She said
that every day we were together

was like re-learning the hard way
she was allergic to shellfish.

Puzzle

The call informing me of mother's death
comes while I'm doing a word search.

I'm no good at those, or Boggle or Scrabble.
I can't make sense of random letters.

It's like when you stop chopping carrots
to stare at your thumb, not sure what it's for.

aiting

In hospital the seasons work in silence.
Here is winter, now on night shift,

gingerly applying a gauze of snow
to a patch of burn-coloured leaves.

Home

Just once, could I come home to an obsequious bellhop
waiting to walk my luggage through a voluminous lobby,

one with a jubilant chandelier and a fountain of koi
that are gentle and forbearing like retired parish priests?

2022 Don Gutteridge Poetry Award
3rd Prize

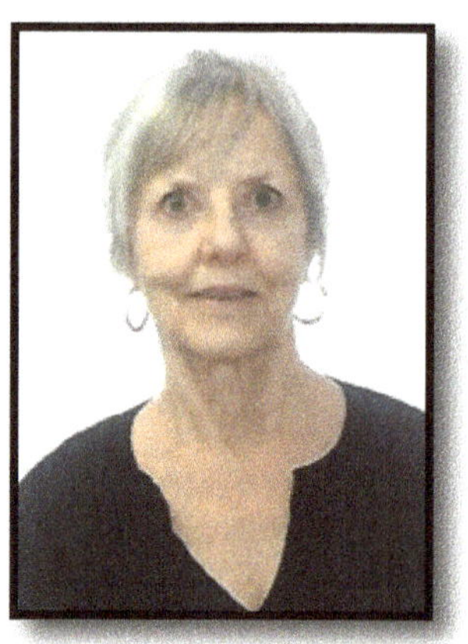

Title: *Seasonal Adjustments*

Author: **K.V. Skene**

ISBN: **978-1-989786-82-6**

Publisher: **Wet Ink Books**

Purchase copies at — www.WetInkBooks.com
or Amazon.ca or Amazon.com

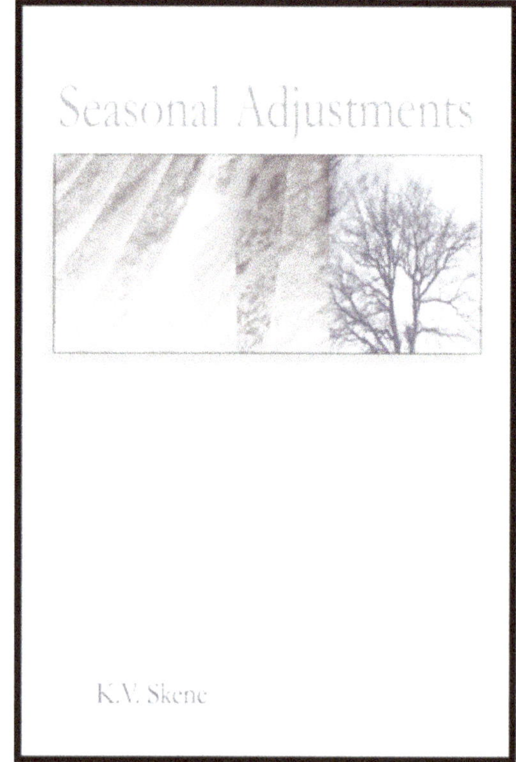

Forward in Time and Space

the wings of a crow
rake the March wind

the following rain
its slow awakening

we walk winter grass and mud and feel
the earth breaking

wherever we go in darkness
or daylight

the bones of history (so old
they've turned to stone)

lie buried beneath altars
rites of passage

from one era
to another – from one life

to another (our little minds
our complex madness, our sad philosophies)

doubly precious
is the child in the womb, the woman

on the bus being carried forward
in time and space

only to be overwhelmed by the connections
between us

drawn by the season
by what we evolved with

the way each heart beats faster
in flight

And Every Year …

i.   As spring rains all over you

> you find yourself water
rushing the culvert and you find the river,
become river (because it's home)
and all who live along it
know its name
> and yours and all that you did
(or did not do) is river, part of the landscape
as each day bursts its filmy sky,
pain already in the wind and
birds are singing
> and singing hurts (more than silence)
more than the danger of burst bank and levee,
long wash of spring flood and every year
you pray you'll escape and every year
you find yourself water …

ii.   Just another overheated summer and you

> awake to the alarm
of the clock (in imperfect light)
and the hills on fire, wind-
burnt sky, grey smoke
suspended …
> admit it's ridiculous –
you've hijacked a god who can
(and does) cremate a landscape,
track black carbon footprints
over your heart
> and you are only one
amongst a multitude (neither saint
nor sinner) called into a world
where even He is not above
flouting the protocol.

iii.   Open autumn to empty air and

            the god-like power of wings,
of sky (litmus paper blue)
and you (white bird) loving its emptiness –
no control, no shadow, no sign
pointing anywhere
            and then it seems impossible
to be following this road –
every house, every tree, every sidewalk
(where you are most at home)
shedding daytime heat.
            Nothing can come of this
(unholy event) you say one day
but what you thought could never come
has fallen, a ripe apple
into your hand.

iv.   And you unmap the cold caves of winter

            where everything has been born
in the dark (yourself and myself) in the hour
before dawn and a shiver runs through
while the world's at its coldest –
hearts beat rapidly
            whenever/however we lose
(moment by moment) our network of blood-
kinship and comrades-in-arms and god-myths,
insist the past is a dead-and-buried land
yet somehow familiar
            like fresh snow on a street
full of bitter silence that is not beginning
(not ending) and even that door slam,
small voice helloing, car revving,
can't find its sound.

A Logical Explanation

gives nothing away, no reason, no rationality
but I keep reimaging a phantom half-life,

my once-upon-a-time life – so light-as-air
I almost missed it in the awakenings

of early morning coffee and toast
and the solitary trek to the first train

and the soft evening's return home
brim-full of skies that spilled

rain upon trees and roofs and empty parks
that ran all the way back

to a childish irrationality underestimated
in the suburban undergrowth,

an obsolete way of being, a serendipitous
long-long-ago

when we were above and beyond happy
had total control over the background

music – a logical explanation of our time/
space/belief in nothing

before everything – snakelike
swallows itself up and ends nowhere

and everywhere in our city, our home, our room,
our wide-open windows …

This Summer the Rain Told Us

water falls because it must
and there is always too much
or too little

wrung out of cumulonimbus, raking
the eaves of exhausted buildings, leached
through drains and gutters

and lakes and ponds choked with grayling
perch and trout and roe and reed and the weed-knit
bodies of suicides and the murdered

and the accidentally drowned
still down among the bottom-feeders and
we are afraid

monsoons usually
arrive too early
or too late

and rivers cannot catch up,
no matter how far they come, no matter
how long the run-off

at the mouth where tides are predictable
and the ocean licks them up
as does the moon

whatever it told the rain and this summer
the rain told us
all the things we never listen to.

Out of the North Wind

a voice you almost remember –
spit-soft vowels, introverted
consonants curl the tongue.
You taste the strawberry ices
of childhood, bite through
the city-wired synapses in your brain
that blur the murmurs of the multitude
and listen closer and closer
to the whole human zoo – singing
while white skulls rattle
and roll around their last days,
while bellies ache
with unfulfilled potential
they drone dank lullabies
and lie awake
humming the animal that furs their bones
and you're blown
back. Before your throat was cut. Back
to the first time
you opened your mouth,
howled
at the crumbling moon.

Over All Things a Whiteness

The fog. The freezing fog.
The unknowable *No*
of November, the whiteness
that never completely covers up

the lies we knead like dough,
let rise and shape and bake and share
en famille
November born and named

one autumnal child at a time fills our house,
breathing as we breath,
our future crystal
clear as that first V flinging itself southwards

and that last desperate yelp of fox
rises out of a seasonal crowding
of mid-life crises.
We have more doubts than grey hairs,

more fears than birthdays
uncovered in the gelid geometry
of bodies slipping from lip
and cup in the absence

of a frost moon, low-lying light. Nothing
waits upon nothing – now
that it's much too late. Now
that it's November.

Cold Comfort

the first winter starts with our shoes
as mornings focus on toes and fingertips

bite down if we look too long
the day will fool us and snow

will fall and paper leaves and pine needles
rise over whitened rooftops

frost-rimed foxes scavenge
in bins and tender wrens hungrily

berrying the bitter holly
take what is theirs

of course, the weather worsens
we have known children

not unlike ourselves
who fail to follow their footprints

all the way back home
but we are quietly confident

January's old moon
pins everything in place

a kiss trapped between two mouths
can ripen in fresh fallen snow

and one of us falls backwards
grows the wings of an angel

one of us
has never been this way before or since

And for Those who Care for Winter

Frosted windows and your fingernails
scratch an initialled heart,
a pinhole camera
while the slow-going traffic whitens
in front of you. A paperweight
where February can be buried
under a snow moon you have seen
in so many cities
that you have ceased to wonder if winter comes
from clouds or mountain ranges
or the roofs of office towers or
treetops …

              Over a thousand miles from there
to here, a blizzard of memories, a drift
of regrets, a cold country
you're still fool enough to believe
is beautiful.

Spring has an Agenda All its Own

and all the short-sleeved wonder of it
is in that handful of blossoms,
the few birds
we know by name
and the gentle greening of the city,
warm rain
washing the kitchen window,
the southwind following
clock-forwarding day –
that persistent peddler
with a backpack of promises
we always buy into.

2022 Don Gutteridge Poetry Award
Honourable Mention

Title: *Titch*

Author: **Kate Marshall Flaherty**

ISBN: **978-1-927396-28-5**

Publisher: **Piquant Press**

Purchase copies at — www.piquantpress.ca

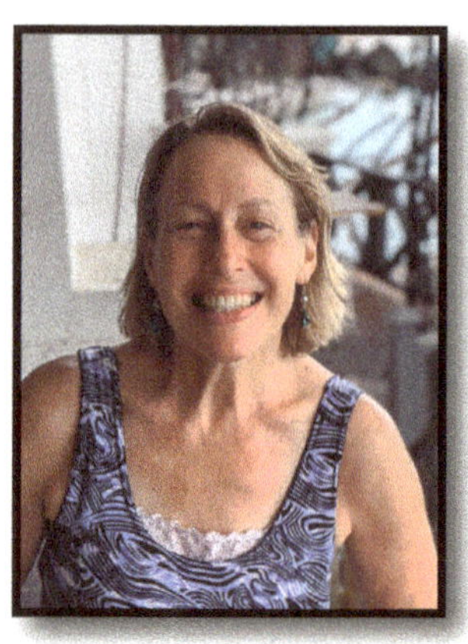

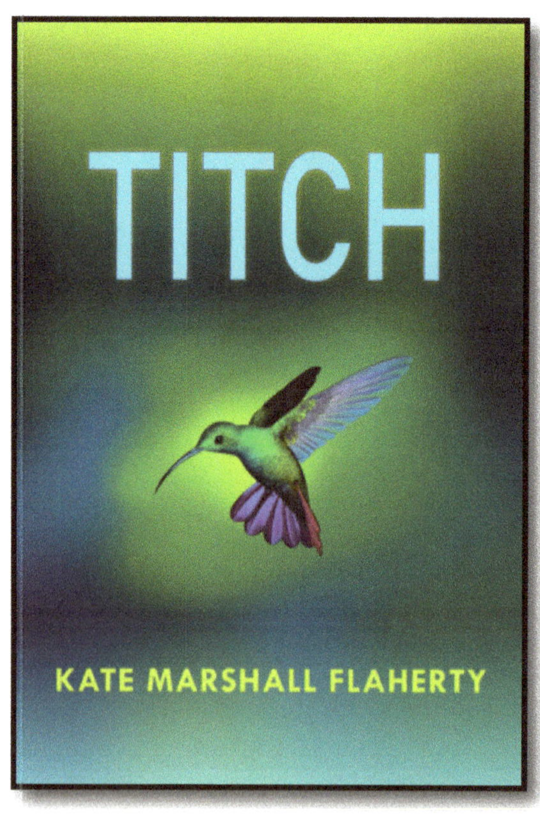

Canoe —

Carib word for dugout,
        Arawak for slender craft,
paddle-propelled,
        birch-bark or cedar,
    wooden ribs,
seated gunnels

slip of narrow boat
        through liquid,
lightweight, fish-shape—

keel-less vessel, we are
        in water, but not wet—

beneath the bay
shimmering shadows dart
and gather

a dragonfly alights

        our J-strokes smooth,
maple-wood paddles
        shellacked and shiny
in summer sun

dip and slide and swing—
little droplets in a line—

the rise of rock in the distance,
a scraggle of pine on the island

        … gulls and clouds dot the sky …

as we pull and glide in unison,
as we pull and glide in silence,
        the island in our sights

the V-trail from our stern settles,
            in our wake

http://bit.ly/3GECCmR

Promise

Feel your fingers along the bark
of the old jack pine by the door;
half-way up you'll find a key
twisted on a rusty keychain, hanging
from a branch.

When you fit the key
in the green porch door, open it
and to the right will be a switch,
under the cowbell.

When you turn on the floodlight,
you'll see the platter of pond,
its bulrush edges leaning
towards the frog-brown water
that smells of clay and catfish.

You can find the wire loop
on the post for the chicken wire
circling the iced pond. Lift the loop,
enter.

Tonight the moon wanes
above the trees. If you listen
to the snow-still scene,
you'll hear a lone wolf
baying at the bright slice.

If you breathe in the March
pond air, you'll taste
a tinge of thawing straw, the clue
as to where the nest is.

You know that geese fly south,
as do great blue herons,
so why this winter nest?

Snap a piece of frozen bulrush
and you will see a bit of fluff,
sinew stalk, but also
glistening moisture—
a sign.

You've seen the newspapers say
the groundhog saw his silhouette,
but this, this sap-in-stalk,
this nest in soggy snow,
the unseen ring around a cuticle moon—
Nature is leaving traces.

The Jack Pine

for dancer Meiko Ando

I skitter over hot rocks,
curl my city-soft toes to grip
smooth sedimentary
like the thirsty trees that cling to
soil-less striations of history.

As a child I saw Tom Thomson's art, Jack Pine
fierce against a sailor-warning sky,
her bent spine leaning into cloud-lines.
It made me wonder what she would do
if unearthed.

I danced summers on group-of-seven rocks,
imagining the wind-reaching Jack Pine,
leaping as she might
if her roots could let go
their talon-grip.

Silhouetted against sunset rose,
I *became* her, uprooted—
able to skip across stone,
sprinkling cone-buds on the shoreline—
lifting my limbs to the wind.

http://bit.ly/3KnRreE

Rose Quartz

Veins of Canadian Shield
cut through sedimentary rock—
blushing against
storm-cloud grey—

streaks of sparkle
in a ridge of rock.

The white pines hold their ground;
tenacious roots grip coastal crags

as gulls lift their piercing cries
above the branch-brooms
whisking away cirrus clouds.

Pink quartz, not white
as chickadee bib or bulrush pulp,

but a flush in a harsh landscape,
a bit of rose in rock's hard history.

http://bit.ly/3o6yAgK

salmon—

i am shimmer-skinned,
spawning   flecks of red,
    shiny-finned,
          i flick
      my gills wide for breath
and wriggle
      side to side in fresh water

i must swim up against
smoothed rocks, the current,
splashes and curls of small rapids   that
gush
          fresh water through me

i am counter-current;   push
up against downspouts
    and falls,
          i fall
back, fin on tail, tumble in trying
and trying to jump
          out of my skin-river,
up the waterfall
                pounding me down

dorsal-finned and spine-supple,
i can do this—
can thrash   against
      the backwards tide

flipped
      and frantic,

          i right
myself, sparkle
      in droplets and spray—
crescent-curve,
                wrestle
                    against water weight

to spawn,
      lay and leave
            my golden roe—

Amending

*For M.F. ***

I say, "Let's go *poem* people

in Union Station –"
You are quiet a moment.

In the great hall's echo, you
whisper,

"I am
a black man. I cannot

startle a traveler
Not even with a poem."

I pause, speechless;
make the ASL sign for *sorry:*

a soft fist
rubbed on the chest.

My fist rubbed on my chest, sore
from the long, backwards track of this.

*To poem: to stop a person and offer to read them a poem

God's Bits of Wood

She is not the long birch pole Deda carved,
not a ticking wheel for measuring steps—

not a "tool thing" at all.
walking stick—

she's a living stem of a bug,
a sapling insect,

her hopping busy bark,
match-thin

she genuflects,
rubs her twig hands together

as if before a feast
or sacred ablution—

No wings, nor honeycomb eyes,
no beetle gloss nor stinger

This bug is bipedal—she, like me, just
wood wisps in the huge forest—

Vultures

There you are, three bald hags,
hunched over and conspiring, high
on the wire above me.

You seem peckish today,
you flesh-eating dementors,
preening and poking black
tar-paper wings.
Valkyries, stay

on the line, don't descend.
My heart burns; I forbid you
down-swooping and carrion-
lust, I deny you access
to my stance on this road.

Silent, red-tipped sisters
with hangover eyes
and wicked kyphosis,
I banish you thricely
your spin, measure, cut!

I, too, have seared with baldness—
puked vomit, my yellow flesh
baggy as sackcloth; I've picked at
bone-splinters, unfurled my bedspread
wingspan. I know

you are hungry, lust
after rot-flesh and things gone bad—
you smell what is nearly dead, and me,
I am threading a string
of words now,

measuring
the distance between us—

2022 Don Gutteridge Poetry Award
Honourable Mention

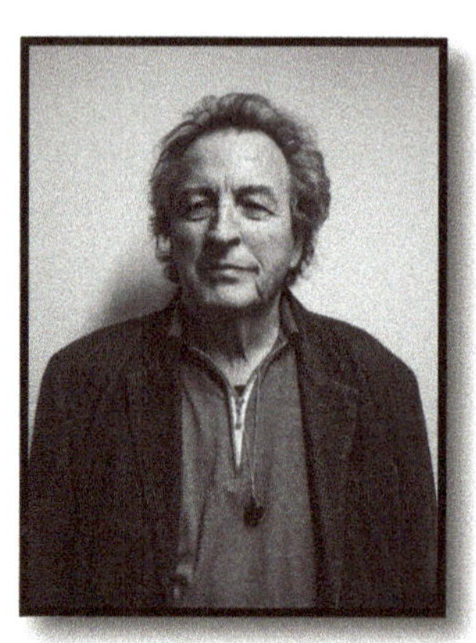

Title: *still arriving*

Author: **Bruce Kauffman**

ISBN: **978-1-989786-81-9**

Publisher: **Wet Ink Books**

Purchase copies at — www.WetInkBooks.com
or Amazon.ca or Amazon.com

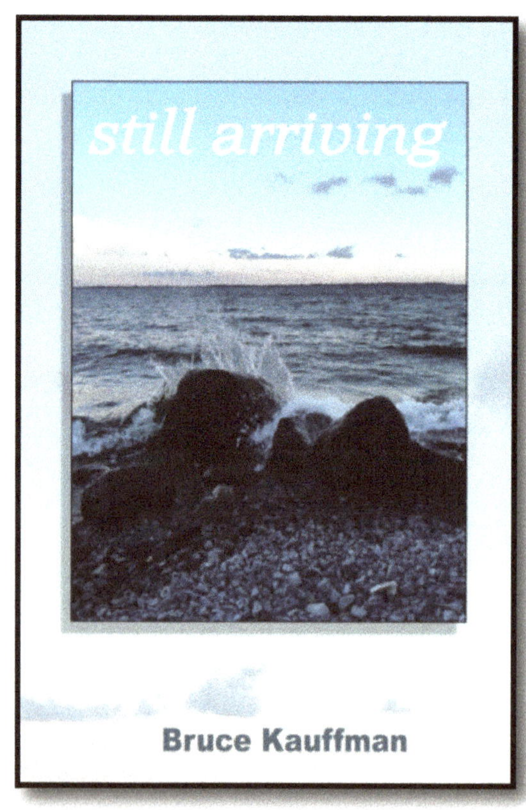

unfinished notes from a journal   (# 6)

July 2019

there is a melancholy rain
outside my window
this evening and
i realize as i write
       that i hold an unguided
       pen in my right hand
its ink as fragile
       as it is indelible

light

in the right light
of day
    and self
even wall
becomes
    mirage

a crossing in a city

as you and i stand
downtown
at an intersection
two main streets crossing

cars   trucks   buses
in all their colours pass by
swarms of pedestrians
in their slow crawl
        on either side

you watch transfixed
by it all
        its flowing colours
        shapes

        and voices

i look at you smiling
embracing it all
and want to tell you
how foreign all of this
        is to me
but cannot

i stand here with
but a language
you have already forgotten

autumn

we all
in an autumn
of our days

not simply any autumn
instead perhaps
       that final one

we
on an earth of soil and stone
built our glass cities

and when then for us
glass was not enough
we made them mirror
       and became them

an offering

not prayer

simpler
       perhaps

a statement
request
a word of thanks

to god   or gods
energy   or universe
to a wavering agnostic belief

to that spirit of endless time
       without time

to the known
the unknowing
the unknowable

to softness
in a world of too little of it

epiphany

for this poet
        this late in life

a reminder that
lesser writ
those morning and vibrant poems
        of youth
instead now
these evening and mourning poems
of and to
        the dead
        the dying

another day

billowy clouds
loosening
narrowing   thinning

throwing out slender
fingers of themselves
reaching
seeming haphazard
but instead prescribed
        directed
        attached

to a deeper blue sky
they stretch their patterns

i watch
reading their global messages
     like tea leaves in a cup

in a day

in a day it will be over

in 24 hours
you will be standing
or sitting still
in this very spot
and unbeknownst to you
everything you know
will have been undone

you will not notice
even one in an infinitude of
incremental changes
in each and every thing

we barely realize surface
never fully recognize
how absolute is process

and in it all
how quickly
        time moves

how slow
        the evolution

difference

of profound difference

asked to sit and
when prompted then to
either create a poem
or allow one

opt for the latter

and there
become not the poet
instead
the ink
       the page

old yellow school bus

perhaps more humility
than economy
and without a
limo'd pretentiousness
an old yellow
school bus approaches

a sheet of white typing paper
taped to the bottom of
its front windshield
near the door

and hand-printed in
bold black ink
with letters large enough
to be easily seen
by anyone even twenty feet away

were simply these words:
        "MacMillan Wedding Party"

Poems by Don Gutteridge
the Canadian Prince of Poetry.

Tagging Along
For my father in loving memory

My Dad lets me tag along
on a cold March morning
while he sets his muskrat traps
in the wind-whetted shallows
of Mitchell's Bay, placing
each baited barb
below the water-line,
just so (like a card-shark
carny beguiling the marks)
where the hapless rodents,
coming up for air and a bite
of breakfast, find themselves
to be the bitten, their silken
coats agleam in the sunlight
that warms their passing, their velvet
pelts destined to be draped
on milady's homely shoulders.

Berry-Bright

For Tom in loving memory

In a long-forgotten drawer
I find this full-colour
photo of you at a year
and a tad, straddling your berry-
bright Tonka (because
your plump unseasoned legs
had yet to weave or waddle),
but now you can locomote
across our cedared deck
like a duck on rollers and honk
your horn like a gaffed goose
to clear the clutter, and in
your eyes is all the laughter
that fifteen months of loving
allows, and the grin you give me
is all pluck and beguiling
gumption.

The Gift

For Anne in loving memory

The pelvic pouch was meant
to keep the foetus firmly
in, but doubled as a cradle
for my lust that softened it
into something akin to love,
and in the tender tangling
of our bodies and the enthused fusion
of our flesh was the world amazed
and we viewed it spinning,
like an infant's dreidel, thru the gift
of the other's gaze.

All Hallows

Point Edward: October 30, 1944

It was Halloween eve, and there
we were chanting ah-
ki-lahs and counting cub-
badges on our cub-green
beanies and bobbing for apples
in a buckled tub, and on
my way home I was surprised
to find myself hobbling,
my left ankle pinched
stiff, prismed with pain,
and by the time I stumbled
onto Grandfather's lawn,
my body was alive with something alien and striving,
and the first fingerlings of fever
blistered on my brow —
and it would be one
heart-harrowing night
of sulfa-suffusions and seven
months abed and adrift
in my dreams before I found
my sea-legs again
and danced home on Al
Hallows Eve.

Jinned

O how we loved to run
with the wind bevelling our backs,
dishevelled in our hair, the girls
beside us with their long-legged
allure and antic prancing,
and if our arms were wings,
we would fly like Icarus
too close to the sun
just to feel the fathoms
of our freefalling bodies,
our bones afloat in the flotsam
of their flesh, and here, where the sky
thrives, we are glad to be guests
of the gods and like the poets
of old, go mad in the wind-
jinned, fancy-fed
fury of their making.

Litmus

What I remember most
about the War, besides
the empty chair at suppertime
where, I was told, my father
would someday sit in his blue
tunic and buffed brass,
or the pink Savings stamps
that wouldn't stick for a nickel
or a dime, or gathering milk-
weed floss to keep
a sailor's jacket jaunty
with its feathered flotsam,
was my Gran in the downstairs
kitchen, all the windows
blacked against the ever-
hovering Hun, knitting
three-needled Argyle
socks for her overseas
sons (and an extra pair
for a best buddy) to keep
their toes from tingling and their hearts
cozied, her lips moving,
stitch by numbing stitch,
as if in penitent prayer
or some ancient incantation
of mothers everywhere to the gods
who suffered their sons to bleed
and perish beyond the healing
litmus of their love.

Balm

Every evening when I was a
summer shy of seven,
before my bed could claim me
for sleep, I would slip downstairs
to say "sweet dreams"
to my Grandpa, and found him,
as ever, at ease in his soft-
bottomed rocker, the only
light in the room, that which
seeped in from the kitchen,
where Gran was counting stitches,
and the hunched console in the corner
with the orange throb in its throat
was pouring out the dreadful
news of the day, and I wondered
if his thoughts were drifting
towards the long-ago war
he'd weathered or the one on the radio,
where his sons now fought –
beyond the balm of his loving.

Strewn Ruins

Point Edward: 1947

When Parson Bell's manse
blew up like Little Pig's
straw abode, scattering
lath and plaster and stricken
bricks everywhere at once,
and we arrived five minutes
behind the fire brigade
in time to see the dust
settle like a dancer's petticoats,
we thought of bomb-bursts
on the Somme or the slow explosion
of a hand-tossed grenade
or perhaps some boulder-buckling
ruckus in Hell, and wondered
idly whether the match
intended for cigarette or cigar
was still attached to the man
who lit it.

Toddler Logic

For Tim

Long before you could read
a word or tell a Jedi
from a gerbil, you could
recite the opening spiel
from *Star Wars,* as if
you had written it yourself
as a favour to George Lucas,
and although it was set in a
galaxy far far away,
there was something in the
lightsaber's slash
and moon-dodging rockets
and cloak-robed Obi
and Buddha-browed Yoda
and the ever-devious Darth
that appealed to your toddler-logic,
while mine was a tepid tour
with the likes of Buck Rogers
in his space togs, or blond-
locked Flash Gordon
or Dick Tracy's flickering
wrist or Mandrake flogging
magic with a cut of his cape,
but boys everywhere, then
or now, with their dewy-eyed
zeal, will always be dazzled
by the glamour of galaxies far
enough away to be real.

The Music of Their Meaning

When I was almost two,
words still floated like flotsam
about the dizzied drum
in my ears, unattached to
anything that mattered, but when
they did so, their syllables sang
of infant selves and home,
and I gorged on the music of their meaning,
suspecting, even then,
that the limit of my lexicon would be
infinite, and any rhymes
to be forged in the fury of their flexing
would poem the world.

Poems by John B. Lee
the 2022 Don Gutteridge Poetry Award
finalist judge.

Stronger in Broken Places

*"The world breaks every one and afterward many are strong at the broken places.
But those that will not break it kills. It kills the very good and the very gentle
and the very brave impartially. If you are none of these you can be sure it will
kill you too but there will be no special hurry."*

Ernest Hemingway from A Farewell to Arms (Chapter XXXIV)

out there
just beyond the edge of ice
where the blue beauty of moving water
begins to shoulder over
the white line
is the very place
where the boy was lost
to the slow shrug
of a seventh wave
shawling up
and shivering over
his small body
with an undulating drag
like wet chain
as link by shuddering link
the cruel-fingered lake
became a last seduction
of foam and frozen froth
and a shaken jigger
of shattered ice
sizzling in the deep beyond all reach
like embers hissing
as they die

and he was swept away
waving as an old horizon
might wave in distant shores that receive
the dying light of day

and I wonder then
are we also
stronger in broken places
as we are
when snapped bones knit

if we ask the threadbare spirit
where it's worn most thin
by the big questions
we are sometimes used to ask

on the wall at home
I have a photograph
of a Cuban father
standing tall beside his little son
their hands both linked in loving
their shadows cast
dark tracings on the sand
as they regard
the beauty of the Caribbean Sea
and what receives the light
in everything
lies just beyond their reach

... *the lover's lament*

I want the human heart
to be so arrow struck
by the whispering
of quivers
coming home in the flesh
that it thickens like a reed fletched pond
an Eros
of an inbreath
exhaled above a sighing bottle mouth
and the vowel sound
of liquid
washing inward
into fluted glass
like the slip of silk on silk
where Cupid hovers
like a darning needle dragonfly
rising and falling and flitting in fascination
with his own and only
iridescent green reflection
in the dark wet looking glass of a long morning
where the sky
flies past beneath the sky
and the mirror
goes deep and deeper still
in two directions drowning down
and drowning upward
like the thought of rain

I want the slight
metallic fragrance
of the milting film
of ovum-coated blue
where flesh meets flesh
in spring
while the peeper frogs

cry out in singing hallelujahs
to the day
and the turtles clack their shells
like wave-rocked stones
as under the fire pit
the blind earth
breaks its silence
where the sowbugs crawl

enough of war
and the so-called two-sided arguments
of a falling out
of families and former friends
enough of the jaded by life
elders
grumbling over grievances
enough of disappointed
expectorations
and coughing in the morning
after dreaming through the night

After My Own Heart

what of yesterday's light
or last evening's darkness
with my hand
to my own living breast
with its resonant breathing
like an old trunk
full to the latches
with grandfather's clothes

I recall how
once I was a young boy
riding the high harvest
of summer hay
under the shadow sweep
of low branches
coming home from the farm
in the village
on our way to the farm on the hill
and we'd stop
to take our ease
and slake our thirst
with the orange-flavoured ice
that wept over the hand
in the heat
oh sweet confection
consumed in the dappled
chiaroscuro of green heaven
as though the breeze in the leaves
were the brush stroke of beauty
laving a water-cooled canvas

it was ever thus then
as it is now with these lines
that follow after my own heart
like the blue-veined flowing
of muffler-cap chatter
and idleness in the fields of tomorrow
to feel both
the empty wagon and
the full-load pull
at the draw bolt tongue of the tractor

what works best
is a better illusion
of luminous dreaming
the one where everyone
lives on forever
like a dead poet's sonnet
of the ochre palm
that leaves its lifeline
deep oh deep
in the earthen darkness of a close at hand cave

And for All the Walking Away

the day
my uncle Russ declined
to turn a gift of earth
upon my mother's ashes
I thought
of the white sand cross
adrift on sacramental oak
what also wets
the vicar's thumb
to bless a child
that puzzlement you see
on an infant brow
I also saw in him
as he said to me
"I'd rather remember her
as she was"
as we who have also felt
the ploughman's grief
at the turning under
of the living green
as though it were
nothing but a spade's worth
of sorrow
to bury a single season
in our wake
and for all the walking away
we've done since then

God Bless the Beauty of all Broken Things

God bless the beauty of all broken things
lost shambles of an autumn shade
where garden asters bloom and cold
chrysanthemums remain
like threadbare buttons
of a tattered coat
grandmothering the earth's
closed over loam
where winter sets its frost
upon a shattering of
etiolating crimson
veined in rust
unhook the stays of summer
watch the apple rot
where wizening is redolent
as wine gone off the cork
what's fruit spoil
to the lazy hive
the omnobibulous butterflies
drink deep surrendering their wings
like breath on silk gone still
there's truth in fading
truth in fog
an energy that dampens light
the soul is like a heart's blush
in the flesh
let fall the lamp harp
and the veil
let fall the drifting night
the angel of the last leaf
lingering in rain
the areola wet with milk
all wakeful stars await
the absent dreamer
whispering of *this* …
the way a word once present
on the tongue
might please both mother
and the satiated lamb

Listening Blue

how like child in prayer
this squirrel
as by the cupping of hands
he is turning each worshipful seed
brought to his mouth
like the single bead
of a broken rosary
cracking the shell
then dropping the dross
in a bountiful tray
this being
the metaphysical hunger
of every spirit
this wanting
of supplication
from the appetite
of the animus of the animal soul

and I'm reminded
of my friend
the poet Roger Bell
breaking open and spitting out
each salted shell
accumulating in his palm
like the heaping of ashes
as we talked together
all those years ago
when we were both young
to the learning of life

and I also think of the field
full with enfilade of those monkish
big-headed flowers
that had followed the sun
all summer
bowing their bent-stalk faces
to the earth
as though humbled
by the divine presence
at a time of holy harvest

what begins in the sacred hold
of each lifeline
that ovum that is us
in silent reverence
to the flavours of sorrow
and the quiet joy it brings
to remember
the almost listening *blue*

Essays on the

2021

Don Gutteridge Poetry Award Winners

by

MSc Miguel Ángel Olivé Iglesias

Foreword

Exceptional Canadian poet John B. Lee wrote, "Great literature broadens our knowledge, deepens our understanding, clarifies our emotions, and connects us to the inner wells of the self where deep need is served. In great literature we also find a meaningful connection with our fellow humans." I have often used this quote in my writings, either academic or literary, to put forth an unquestionable truth, the profound significance and influence of literature in everyone´s life. It endows us with knowledge, allows us to reach an insightful and creative construal and reassessment of our worldview, ignites sundry emotions in us—and creates/fosters human bond, human exchange, which is central to survival and growth, to meaningfulness, aesthetics and ethics.

Reading Canadian literature has become a necessary part of my life. I have been doing that for a few years now, immersing in the rich motifs and contribution writers have offered making their work both proudly Canadian and deservedly universal. I was attracted as well to the pleasurable act of reviewing many of those writers thus paying my personal tribute to CanLit.

A tireless promoter and champion of Canadian literature is publisher, poet, photographer, artist Richard M. Grove, who in collaboration with another iconic poet, Don Gutteridge, generated the *Don Gutteridge Award*. The year 2022 stands as the inaugural year for the award with Gutteridge as the sole judge.

Grove asked me to write a few intro words about Don, the Award and the first group of poets to win it. Four authors received the 2022 Don Gutteridge Award. Besides Don´s wise, experienced opinion to select them, it is my modest contention that the names we will be reading in this book have left a permanent mark on Canadian poetry.

But, let´s talk about the judge first (you can read my review on him in the book). Don Gutteridge's attitude towards life and poetry is evidenced in his poem "Defy": "Poetry is both bliss and consolation, a way of speaking to the world that subsumes both shy and defy." Notice how Don considers poetry to be *communication*, a principle I introduced with Lee´s quotation. Gutteridge understands that poems speak to people, they state something, they grant happiness in the realization of the self, and bring comfort to the poet's soul, other qualities of writing explained by Lee.

In an interview with Don via email when I was preparing to write my book *Five Canadian Poets: Analytical Essays on James Deahl, John B. Lee, Don Gutteridge, Glen Sorestad, A. F. Moritz,*(QuodSermo Publishing, 2021), I asked him if he thought he would ever give up writing poetry. His answer was definitive: "Nothing short of a stroke could stop me from writing poetry… I seem to dream poems and wake up writing them... I am very fortunate that the Muse has never let me down."

Read his piece "Ruthless" to absorb fully the depth of his answer and his indefatigable pursuit of truth as his ultimate goal when he warmly *enlinks* words in his lines:

> *And me composing poems:*
> *inklings I tease*
> *towards some sense*
> *in words whetted upon*
> *the wheel of memory*
> *and swerving askance*
> *upon the page where they lean*
> *upright, enlinked,*
> *ready to be swallowed whole,*
> *raw and ruthless*
> *in rhythmic pursuit*
> *of the truth.*

When we read his work, we find, we sense, all his experiences outlined, elaborated on, colored in the excellent penmanship we enjoy across his oeuvre. This is the judge, the man—*the bard*, as I have called him. This is the name honoring the Award.

The four winners, whom I will talk about in the book too, are now linked to an important award that will continue to group fine Canadian writers. All four winning books will be published by Wet Ink Books.

First Place: $2,500.00
David Blaikie – *A Season in Lowertown.*

Second Place: $1,000.00
Wendy Jean MacLean – *On Small Wings.*

Third Place: $500.00
Antony DiNardo – *Through Yonder Window Breaks.*

Honourable Mention:
Mike Madill – *The Better Part of Some Time*

In my book *Five Canadian Poets…*, I said that those five poets (Don included), "as contemporary Canadian poets of such high standing, are the style that future poets will emulate, they are the model that others will imitate and follow. They are future Al Purdys, future Milton Acorns, future Dorothy Livesays. They are the best fountain to drink from in the inexhaustible Canadian spring." I am positive that Blaikie, MacLean, DiNardo and Madill can be counted –in fact, by winning the Award they already are on the right path– among those poets who will emulate greats like Deahl, Lee, Gutteridge, Sorestad and Moritz. I toast to that thought.

Don Gutteridge:
The Poet Who Seems to Dream Poems and Wakes Up Writing Them

An understanding of the significance of Canadian poet Don Gutteridge may start by reading the following: "Literary critics will have much to say about Gutteridge's uniquely Canadian vision. I am content that his poetry is accessible, unobtrusive, delights the ear, stirs the heart and even enters into the soul. It is the art that mirrors inner life". These are the words of R. G. Moyles, (The University of Alberta. In The Journal of Canadian Poetry).

The first part tells us of a "unique Canadian vision". Hallelujah. Gutteridge is *par excellence* one of those gifted people who grasp with mastery the Canadian concept, maximize it and manifest it in their writings. Read his poem "**Dunes at Canatara**" about which I said was *Purdian* in spirit:

> *It took a million years*
> *to sculpt these dunes,*
> *grain by grain of wavewashed sand whipped*
> *by seasoned winds into*
> *voluptuous curves*
> *and bevelled runes.*
> *It took my pals and me*
> *an afternoon to put*
> *our imprimatur upon*
> *the shimmering concavities,*
> *our bodies pressing*
> *their wry signatures deep*
> *deep into the sun-stunned sand,*
> *feeling the heat of a hundred*
> *centuries oozing through.*

The second part of Moyles´s quote tells us of the quality and characteristics of his poetry: "accessible, unobtrusive, delights the ear, stirs the heart and even enters into the soul". Moyles is pointing out the ease with which readers can enter and walk through Gutteridge´s poetry.

Nothing will stand in the way between them and the poet, no inextricable paths, no obscure rhetoric, no jumbled, superfluous overdoing of the line and the meaning. Beyond that, features that mark great poetry in English – rhythm, which is ear-comforting, power, which is heart-reaching – are revealed by Moyles. Finally, the feature that makes a poet just one more poet or a transcendent one, like him: Gutteridge´s poetry "enters the soul". Once we read his work, it will unequivocally win our hearts and settle in our innermost niches reserved for great things, those that move the spirit and enlighten us. Enjoy the poems below, where Don sums up his connection with poetry:

Rhymes

In my advancing age
let me still be the one
wrestling with words to wield
the world anew, to send
them dancing on some
distant dais, sylvan
with simile: the page
where all my rhymes ring
true.

Ruthless

> *And me composing poems:*
> *inklings I tease*
> *towards some sense*
> *in words whetted upon*
> *the wheel of memory*
> *and swerving askance*
> *upon the page where they lean*
> *upright, enlinked,*
> *ready to be swallowed whole,*
> *raw and ruthless*
> *in rhythmic pursuit*
> *of the truth.*

But it is Don himself who exposes his own poet´s soul when he said to me in response to a question I asked him: "Nothing short of a stroke could stop me from writing poetry… I seem to dream poems and wake up writing them... I am very fortunate that the Muse has never let me down." He said that for my book *Five Canadian Poets* (QuodSermo Publishing, 2021), and proved his deep bond with poetry as I delved into his life and work and wrote *The Canadian Poet Who Wrote Himself Whole* (QuodSermo Publishing, 2022) in honor to his long-standing career.

Writing about Don, especially the latter book, which was about him, I knew it meant a huge undertaking but a necessary and meaningful one. There is an unobjectionably literary, educational, tasteful, evocative, kindhearted and elegant value in what Don writes. His oeuvre is an invaluable contribution to literature, a treasure in Canadian literary heritage.

I have said before that Don Gutteridge has a singular style, comfortably placed within a latent universality. He is recipient, repository and paradigm at the same time. He is committed to his land, evidenced when we read his poems and notice references to nature, to geographies and seasons, to vast maps of wildlife and wilderness.

In Gutteridge, there is an unavoidable, deeply-ingrained family-friend-wife leitmotif. About his family poems, Emily-Jane Hills Orford said, "Special family connections. The simplicity of treasured family moments..." (Hidden Brook Press release) She added, "I have read a number of Don Gutteridge's poems over the years and I continue to marvel at his ability to capture the simplest of moments in a capsule and make it grander than life with his poetic observations." (ibidem).:

Together

In this photo, my mother
and father, standing tall
on my grandfather's lawn
in their Sunday suits,
hold me up high
between them for the camera's
loving eye, like a prized
doll for all the world
to see, their hands tethered
to steady me on my maiden
shoot, as happy as they
will ever be, and I still
regret I wasn't enough
to keep them together

I have often stated that "Canadian poets exceed in wording, honoring and recalling facts, events, people, and names." Don´s poems invariably state whom they were written for. Particularly moving are the ones written to Anne, his wife, and to Tom, his grandson. Even though sadness is present in the cry of the bereaved man, Don finds consolation in beauty and memories. The poet does not complain or lament forever: he sees a form of healing in writing. Imagery pulses and emanates from Don´s poetry; he handles language tools fruitfully, innovatively. An essential component of the poet´s poetry is the link of rhythm and musicality. Both elements are unavoidable for him, as he told me also while I was writing my aforementioned books.

One stunning example of his love for Anne, his wife, is "Au Revoir". It is a heart-breaking poem. We see a sophisticated poet in love, deeply in love for his departed wife. Everything reminds him of her. Torn in pain and nostalgia, he weaves scene after scene, image after image, glued to the physicality of her memory. Despite grief, he manages to erect a monumental piece here and in other poems, **elegies for my beloved wife**" as he told me once:

> *I do not empty this house*
> *of your presence: you are here*
> *in every room we shared*
> *breath in, your clothes still*
> *hang where they belong*
> *in their closets, and every painting*
> *that adorns our walls is a reminder*
> *of your artist's eye, and the chesterfield,*
> *your bête noir, still*
> *bears your imprint, and a novel*
> *lies where your fingers last*
> *lingered, nor am I made*
> *forlorn on entering the space*
> *now vacant of the woman*
> *I cossetted and cradled with*
> *love in its essence, for we are taught*
> *that death is not an ending,*
> *not goodbye but au revoir:*
> *I refuse that platitude,*
> *preferring your haunting hover*
> *and the remnants of the things you touched*
> *with such tenderness.*

In all his greatness as a poet and person, Gutteridge is a modest human being. Alongside many other Canadian contemporary writers, Gutteridge has left a mark on what I termed in my book *Five Canadian Poets* as **the Canadian style**.

Gutteridge belongs with those iconic writers who dignify the Canadian literary mosaic, who are a part of, as John B. Lee puts forth, the "Great literature" [that] "broadens our knowledge, deepens our understanding, clarifies our emotions, and connects us to the inner wells of the self where deep need is served. In great literature we also find a meaningful connection with our fellow humans."

Don Gutteridge´s writings expand our cognition and understanding of the world, shake and set our own emotions free, and activate our nexuses with ourselves and our innermost urges. Moreover, his poetry comes from his connection with human beings and helps us revisit our own, substantially, indelibly, transcendently. As Christian Sia of Readers' Favorite observed, "These poems are filled with the humanity of the writer and readers can easily relate to the emotions evoked in the lines… " (Hidden Brook Press release)

If at the beginning of these words I suggested readers to start with Moyles´s quotation, now I include a longer critique by John B. Lee, in reference to one of Don´s books, which condenses Gutteridge´s immeasurable quality as a writer: "I read poem after poem and think it is a masterpiece. There is an abiding sadness, but the sadness of wisdom, of knowing that if we live long enough, we lose loved ones, we keep them in our hearts though they are gone. Long ago I coined the phrase "the presence of absence" to capture in as few words as possible what I felt when I thought of those loved ones I'd lost. We preserve them in poems. We keep them alive in memory and dream. We weep and grieve and lament and celebrate. This book is profound and wise and consoling. I will be reading it again and again because it goes deep. It has the courage of autobiography without the honey trap of the confessional." (Hidden Brook Press release)

Gutteridge will never cease to write and wonder at the world inside and outside him. He will always be caught up in the mystery that is putting words and sentences together to create something that is, to him, undefinable.

Unsayable

I've spent a lifetime
seeking the reason for rhyme
in pursuit of the perfect poem
where dactyls dance until
they make indelible sense
in the midst of metrical meaning,
where I find my heart stirred
by the motive for metaphor
in the ept uttering of the un-
word, the saying of what is,
alas, unsayable.

There we go, Don Gutteridge´s poetry is invincible ink and "indelible sense". I invite everyone to toast to the man, the husband, the family man, the father, the friend, the writer, the symbol, the bard. Let´s close these comments about Don with precisely a poem he titled "**Bard**":

I find it hard to imagine
a life without the wizardry
of words: the nuances of nouns
and verbs surging: pinned
in the prism of a poem, where rhyme
has its reasons and rhythm is what
the heart hears in the silence
between beats and simile
has its seasons, and I was born
to pain and poetry, and longed
to embrace the arcane business
of being a bard.

Weeping and Dancing
with David Blaikie's

A Season In Lowertown
1st Prize, 2021

Winner of the Don Gutteridge Award, poet David Blaikie enters my life with poems riding simultaneously wild, free and gentle in his *A Season in Lowertown*, a 2022 book of confessionary spirit that exudes history, involvement, search, blood, "sins", deeds and aspirations nascent and in the making.

His biblical allusions in the Introduction impart an aura of gravitas to what is coming, which readers will feel bound to remember as they start their sojourn along Blaikie´s poetry. Hence, as both reader and reviewer, I felt the urge to pick up his line of thought and state right from the beginning that Blaikie has found in his work "a time to speak" as well.

The poet admits straightforwardly "*I wept in Lowertown, I danced there. It exists within me still…*" Two sides of the soul, two expressions of what makes us human burst in Blaikie, the weeping and the dancing, in a premonition of what we will be reading and experiencing. It will be a confluence of true-to-life emotions sizzling from cover to cover, inviting us to the act of opening our eyes wide, understanding, acknowledging. Maybe Blaikie thinks of the reader as a confessor; therefore, he opens pages of his life and asks to partake—no matter what.

The book is divided into five sections: Flight, Night, Spirits, Netherworld, Moments and Prologue. Trapped in the impossibility of addressing every single poem, I will only touch upon some of them. The first section includes seven pieces from which I comment "Trumpets" first.

The poem unfolds in a million burning thoughts that the poet hurries to jot down. You notice the scurrying reminiscences piling up in utterances, which despite their trepidation, despite the assorted ideas and references, do leave in the reader the contours of an impression: the poem as a psychological rundown of what is going on in the poet´s mind, interspersed by personal, historic, literary, social and cultural slices.

Formally speaking, a conspicuous absence of punctuation marks in the poem contributes to represent the swirling trains of uninterrupted thoughts. This characteristic leaves readers breathless if they attempt to follow the lines, and it makes them recognize the "time to break down" pulsing in the poet and his embracing "the grit and grime…, the bars, the taverns, the all-night diners and hotels with creaking beds" he tells us about in his Introduction.

Let´s quote lines that mirror what I have commented:

> *"… and drank a lot*
> *the bottomless*
> *drinking of being young //*
> *rebellion hissing like a fuse inside*
> *the times blowing trumpets in my ears //*
> *men about to fly to the moon*
> *and put big footprints there*
> *I'm not sure I was thinking*
> *at all, the minister in his collar*
> *so black and white //*
> *doubt swirled like dust inside"*

The second poem in the section, "Blue," presents us a more laid back Blaikie, more imbued with close realities, more *sober*. The poet eases from the turbulence and confusion of "Trumpets" – arguably his *weeping part* – into an almost idyllic remembrance of a moment that led, in his own words, to a significant status in his life – his *dancing* part. "Blue" is a poem that brought back sparks of the well-known song "Heaven" by Canadian singer Bryan Adams: "Once in your life you find someone who will turn you all around." Blaikie words it in his simple, precise, decisive two final lines: *"I told myself I'd settle in / and we walked from there into life"*.

"Blue" offers us a poet who knows how to handle poetic language so readers become witnesses of the scenes he recreates. He explodes in figurative forms that strike home:

> *"… elm trees nodding at an eggshell sky*
> *the river sliding away*
> *her eyes alight*
> *the wind soft in her hair*
> *and that white dress*
> *which sighed so on her body…"*

Blaikie captures the event with uniqueness, using a tender and conclusive hyperbole to limn it, as is seen in line four of the extract below:

> *"… as I stood there*
> *in that quivering air*
> *of cars on summer grass*
> *family, friends, and god*
> *gathered round*
> *and heard her recite each word…"*

Section two, Night, with ten pieces, continues to chronicle Blaikie´s life and doings. From it, "Lowertown" as opener. This is a flash-on snapshot of the town, taken from the poet´s perception. Imaginably gloomy, redolent and resilient perhaps, the poem – high in metaphorical feats – depicts a mental state intentionally exposed and intensely dissected by the poet.

Let´s contemplate this excerpt where well-knit tropes are evident:

> *"the clock wrote shadows*
> *on the walls of Lowertown*
> *pushing the daylight back*
> *in those scrawled out*
> *chalkboard days…"*

Then let´s consider these lines where the poet reveals his thoughts again:

> *"… hardly thinking, hardly sleeping*
> *waiting for night to fall*
> *and set nerves alight*
> *with pangs*
> *of who knows what*
> *just pull down the shades…"*

Finally, let´s trace the transition that occurs from the first fragment to the second and to the one below. We are caught in a sequence moving from apparently settling depictions to a sudden change of pace to a critical outburst in the last segment:

> *"… inject both eyes with neon*
> *and make briefcase interlopers*
> *disappear with their shiny shoes*
> *and business mouths*
> *and every suit*
> *that ever got worn in the name*
> *of politics, god and commerce"*

Obviously, this poem revisits and remixes the thematic theses propounded by Blaikie since "Trumpets."

The section carries on with Blaikie´s journey along his Lowertown season with poems, like "Jail," as samples of those dark periods he went through. This section is rich in overlaps of *weeping* and *dancing*.

Section three, Spirits, features fifteen poems. There is constant reference in Blaikie´s book to a writer of renown, so I directed my attention to the poem entitled "Kerouac." A romantic hero in the eyes of many young people, Kerouac seems to be a compass for the poet.

The poem particularly tells of Blaikie´s remembrances of Kerouac and contexts where he lived and worked. It is a poet honoring another poet and novelist who marked many people´s lives. There is a reference to Kerouac´s trend-setting novel, *On the Road*. See the effervescence with which Blaikie wrote about the novel and its significance to him: *"On the Road was almost holy…"*

Section five, Moments, has fourteen poems. I was especially touched by "Melancholy." A blend of skill and emotion, the poem reflects on one of those sensations that make us "weep or dance" depending on circumstances.

The theme has been approached by many writers and poets. Iconic Cuban singer and songwriter, Silvio Rodríguez, wrote about it: "Oh melancholy, silent sweetheart, intimate couple from yesterday; Oh melancholy, joyful lover, your pleasure always captures me, Oh melancholy, Lady of Time, kiss that comes back like the sea, Oh melancholy, Rose of sigh, tell me who can love me…" Blaikie made Rodríguez's tune resonate in my heart as I read the poem. See what Blaikie feels:

> *"the thing with melancholy*
> *is that it tiptoes in*
> *and then … is there*
> *as if it had not been away*
> *a mist, a thin gray rain…"*

The poet conceptualizes melancholy as an ever-present state, one coming and going like the ebb and flow of sentiments, yet points out that sometimes it is never *actually* gone and resides deep within: "*as if it had not been away…*"

There are Kerouac allusions in still another piece, "Of the Mind." The poem stands as homage recollections beyond the famous Beat Generation novelist. It begins with Lawrence Ferlinghetti, an author Blaikie took the title for this piece from (*A Coney Island of the Mind.* New Directions Publishing, 1958). It mentions other names stamped on the U.S. literary map such as Allen Ginsberg, Joyce Johnson and William Burroughs. But it also sprinkles names of places and locations. I sensed *Purdian* airs in this poem.

The last section, Prologue, has three poems. All three are special in their own right, in their own perspectives and motifs. A romantic myself almost since I was born, I quote, full, his "And After That …"

In respectful disagreement with Shakespeare's belief that "All my best is dressing old words new" (in disagreement because we are quite aware of Shakespeare's greatness and of Blaikie's broad range to masterly treat and blend theme, language and style as if they were on a painter´s palette), and elated in the thereon discovery that images and tropes can be continually renovated, I was moved by this short piece. Enjoy it:

> *"it's said that a man*
> *is never the same*
> *when a woman*
> *has slept in his eyes*
> *and painted her scent*
> *on the skies of his flesh*
> *and swept*
> *lesser wisdoms away"*

His last poem, "The Bridge," pensive, yearning, intimate; a closer *par excellence*, invites us to a recurring theme in every writer, poet and artist. Parting, that "sweet sorrow," is colored by the poet´s keen frame of mind. In an instant, he plays with sublime metaphors again, captures images and memories re-dimensioning them into genuine symbolic evocations, goes back in time and speaks to his beloved one:

> *"below the iron bridge / /*
> *where we stopped and*
> *stood so often, and the sun*
> *would find you there*
> *reach past clouds*
> *above the moody dam*
> *and pour itself upon you…"*

Let´s find endless delight in the lines above, in the whole poem and in the book. Let´s toast to the superb amalgamation of solemnity, cutting naturalness, sheer frankness and sensitivity overflowing them. Let´s "… *hold that / like an old Matryoshka doll / and all the rest will be inside"* and never hesitate to "weep and dance" with a forthright David Blaikie and his *A Season in Lowertown*, a rightfully merited Don Gutteridge Award holder.

Taking Wing on a Million Small Wings
with Wendy Jean Maclean´s

On Small Wings
2nd Place, 2021

Reading Wendy Jean´s intro to the book, her bio and comments on her work, two ideas *fluttered* in my head. First of all, a quote from the Bible, "A longing fulfilled is sweet to the soul" (Proverbs 13:19). Wendy has met her calls and her longings have been fulfilled, so her soul must surely feel sweet. I am so glad she has found *raison d'être* in her life. Her poems are a clear cut reflection of her life and feelings and gift to write. Her inspirational springs flow around and inside her.

Secondly, the "birdful" spirit of the book brought back to me a well-known Canadian birder, Marvin Orbach, whose poetic work I reviewed in my book *In a Fragile Moment. A Landscape of Canadian Poetry* (Hidden Brook Press, 2020). Particularly emotive is Wendy´s own description of how it all started and why: "These winged creatures have provided me with insight into the strange migrations of life and death, and the echoes "round the corner"."

The first poem, "On Small Wings," is deeply touching. It is a gentle prelude to what we, readers, are about to experience. The poet´s exhortation to do what she asks comes to the reader filled with passion and kindness, with latent evidence that the poet knows what she talks about and wants the reader to partake. It is an invitation we cannot refuse. I want to quote it fully:

Be gentle with this moment.
Feel the brush of its wings
as it circles around you.
Hold out your hand with seeds of hope.
When it comes to you, let it rest.
Be still. Hold this wonder.
Be gentle with this moment.
It has far to go on small wings.

This is a poem to tremble with, to be illuminated by. In writing it, Wendy must have thought of everything: short, simple sentences to allow the reader to breathe them and the message in, metaphors that whisper more than speak out loud, words and images that "flirt and flutter, or hide in the shrubbery with lots of jargon and rhetoric…" (from the author´s intro), which she holds in her privileged hands to sprinkle them onto pages and pages.

The poet´s request to do what she proposes will strike home in every reader, as it did in me. On the book´s back cover, Dr. Mark Sirett says, "During this extraordinary time, one can find greatly needed solace, serenity and hope in the words of Wendy Jean MacLean…"

My favorite line – in a completely favorite poem – is "*Hold out your hand with seeds of hope.*" Faith, **hope** and charity echo in it in times of despair, confusion and death. But the author asks to have hope. She asks to fly with it on the "small wings" she spreads for the reader.

Meg Freer said about the book, "Wendy MacLean has written a beautiful tribute to the joy of life…" and Deborah Dunleavy commented: "The spiritual relationship with nature as evident in her poetry inspires the reader to pause and recognize those things which we take for granted: the spring rain, trees, rocks, water, even a spider's web".

If my comments made you think the previous poem is a great poem, be ready to feel the same with "Green me":

Green me in this saturation
of spring rain.
Unfold yourself into this day.
Un-pleat my soul.

Dredge the dreary troughs of ego

where judgement lingers

leaving calcified clichés on fumbling walls

I wish weren't there

The trees laugh at me

surfeited by my vocabulary

when all they need

is rain

to open

to splendour

on this May morning

As I have said of other fine poets, in Wendy we pick a vibrant environmentalist, a poet whose muses come down with and like blessing rain. In my mother tongue, Spanish, *saturation* has a semantic hue suggestive of unnecessary excess. However, when you read *"Green me in this saturation / of spring rain"* there is no trace of excess: you want to tread onto the image, to shower in it or dive into it.

Alongside the environmentalist resonance of the poem, there are airs of a social character that explore the many sides of human nature: *"Dredge the dreary troughs of ego / where judgement lingers / leaving calcified clichés on fumbling walls"*. Dunleavy points out that "Award-winning poet Wendy Jean MacLean offers the reader a moment to pause, reflect and contemplate on the wonderous fragility of life".

The thoughtful, profound woman and her sources of love are revealed as well in a powerful piece, "You Are Continents to Me". The title is embracing and superbly hyperbolic, a notion that is penned along the poem, where Wendy harmonizes *"French valleys and rugged shores / seismic thrusts and tectonic shouts / islands that separate delicate biomes"* with *"a new world / from the porch / a kingdom from the garden swing / a universe of raindrops and tulip bulbs / and the dog sleeping on our bed…"* with the heart-warming closing lines *"I will show you the paths through the forest / as you teach me the ways of the stars"*. All of these realities are masterly, sensitively condensed to tell her husband what she feels, and epigrammatically concluded in the last stanza:

<blockquote>
I am not yours to be conquered
you are not mine to be found
I will show you the paths through the forest
as you teach me the ways of the stars
</blockquote>

One of the many blurbs I read about the book states: "Cosmic and intimate, gritty and gentle: from the first moments of creation to the aching losses of dementia, these poems draw from nature's relentless promises of birth, death and change…" The poem "As I Spend the Night Beside You" speaks of those labyrinths of life and death.

Wendy has worded in sincere, resounding lines what her mother and she went through. An especially graphic start, "*Nothing can make this chair comfortable / but I pretend to rest / as I spend the night sitting here / beside you…*" leads to "*I find comfort being here / when you waken. / "Am I dying?" you ask. / "Not tonight, Mom."* Notice some sort of peaceful aura created when the poet tells us (her mother) that there is relief in being right there when she wakens. It is a sentiment-baring, bonding instant of filial love.

The context makes the poet remember when it was the other way around, when she was born. The endless cycle of life repeats:

<blockquote>
I remember
standing beside my babies' cribs
watching them sleep
counting their breaths.
You did the same
when I was newborn
resting in a hospital bassinette
beside your bed
</blockquote>

The poem "To Let the Day End" is a hymn to life. It is an evocation of eternity, compacted in the very first stanza, an evocation of what life was:

<blockquote>
You will always be young
to those who lost you at your death
But earth welcomes your ancient soul
and waits, with a blanket of soil
for your cradle of bones
</blockquote>

If as readers you have any doubts, move to stanza two:

> *Your family keep a candle, lit*
> *on your grave.*
> *In the strong winds*
> *the light moves and dances*
> *as you moved and danced*
> *in those last days.*

Dunleavy told us that Wendy "… reminds us that we are all a part of a bigger moment, passing though time." That moment comes and goes and as it moves from the mists of time so it scurries into them again:

> *this wind*
> *is the same gusty gift*
> *of breath and spirit*
> *that makes life from death.*

The last two lines of the poem give both sides of the perpetual enigma of life:

> *to let the light flicker*
> *to let the day end.*

I cannot close my comments on the previous poem without bringing to the readers fragments from a poem that Wendy made me wistfully remember. Being the actual author´s name still in dispute, I quote the website source I took it from: https://en.wikipedia.org/wiki/Do_Not_Stand_at_My_Grave_and_Weep

Readers will instantly realize the commonalty of feeling and sanctity in both poems, the assurance that wafts in them, the profound connection that remains. In Wendy´s piece, it is the survivor who speaks; in the poem I quote from, it is the departed one yet signals of faith and hope remain untouched in both. Enjoy Wendy´s poem, Wendy´s book and these segments from "Do not stand at my grave and weep":

Do not stand at my grave and weep,
I am not there, I do not sleep.
I am a thousand winds that blow;
I am the diamond glints on the snow.
I am the sunlight on ripened grain;
I am the gentle autumn's rain.

On Small Wings fills our hearts. I cannot think of more adequate ways to explain the spirituality it is endowed with. Yet beyond and above that inner spirituality fly colossal wings that flit and perch on the soul of every reader. This is a book to cherish and reread every time we are confronted with the riddles of life and death, the brittleness of living and the greatness of reaching out for hope and enlightenment in nature, in the simple things.

Please read *On Small Wings*. You will take flight into what Sirett referred to as "… the profound beauty and transformative power of nature… Like nature itself, her musical words sing truth with a depth of inner joy, harmony and peace."

Inner joy, harmony and peace. This is the balance, the healing prayer, the million wings.

Looking Out Windows
with Antony Di Nardo´s

Through Yonder Window Breaks
3rd Prize, 2021

I have had the privilege of writing and publishing about some of Antony Di Nardo´s previous books. I read and enjoyed *Skylight* and *Gone/Missng*. A poet "always… attracted to nature, as much as to the surreal and the absurd" (his words), Di Nardo invites us once more to his constant experimenting and his unique style to write and play with meanings, words and sentences.

Di Nardo´s take of life and poetry defines him. He clearly states that "a poem should not mean but be." This is what he does when he embarks on his journey *Through Yonder Window Breaks*. His poems ARE ergo they breathe and live. And in the poems, the universe – next to him (inside him) or far beyond – pulses and offers rich meanings even when he says they are not supposed to *mean*.

See these lines from his opening piece, "Bloomsday":

> *Every room*
> *Sufficient to furnish a record of where I have and*
> *Haven't been, a window in each with an inside-out*
> *And a book I put back on the shelf.*

As a reader, I felt the need to step into every room with Di Nardo. Those rooms speak and the poet acknowledges it. Windows seem to have attracted his eyes and set his poet´s mindset in motion. Yet my favorite line is the end line. Di Nardo is an inveterate reader: he puts a book back in the shelf in a cycle I am certain he has been repeating for years.

"A Poem That's More About Me Than Birds", Di Nardo´s second proposal in the book, brings us the interplay of nature and thought, "*I like to watch as much as listen—*". From this initial statement, we travel with the poet and his metaphors ("The banter and bluster of wings painting leaves"), which take us high with the birds and exposes a vibrant, observant poet whose senses absorb what surrounds him.

One of the comments I liked best about the book is the following: "The poems frame reflections, observations, in language that is straight-forward and transparent. Images are layered; the syntax playful…" The notion of a playful syntax merged with an overturning of meanings is noticed in:

> *The tear between two clouds and the sounds I heard*
> *Telling me to wait for the geese to re-appear.*
> *But they don't, not the ones I was expecting—*
> *I've confused the words around my house*
> *With the words inside my head.*

The reader will notice the change of pace, the change in the train of thought and observation of realities outside the poet to a sudden (visually anticipated by —) introspective realization: words inside the poet´s head.

Further down in the book, we come across "Five Selected Scenes of Winter at the Window", piece 1. The curiosity detected by a comment I read, "These poems are curious about the natural world and interested in nurturing a relationship with it", flutters in the brief piece:

> *No bigger than a foot*
> *The sharp-shinned hawk*
> *Falls into my boot*
> *And pulls out a sock*
> *Gripped in its talons*
> *Two shades of yellow*
> *My sock ablaze, the sky*
> *A shocking glow*

We see the poet who watches: "sharp-shinned hawk / Two shades of yellow / sock ablaze, the sky / a shocking glow" – and no full pause at the end of the poem as if there were a continuity of idea and of the infinite expansion of the glow.

Then I came upon piece 3. Somehow Poe (an example of classical influences Di Nardo refers to?), the icon of sounds, echoed in Di Nardo´s play with words and sounds:

> *In the beginning birds*
> *gave us the words*
> *for flitter*
> *and flutter,*
> *for the flute*
> *and flicker of wing tip*
> *to wing tip,*
> *for the long graceful swoop*
> *of a hand,*
> *unfettered,*
> *ungloved,*
> *uncluttered,*
> *turning the page*

And again we appreciate the nature-man back-and-forth, the transition from an outside depiction to the image of a page being turned. In changing vowel sounds, meanings change too in a cycle of freedom of the poet to use expressive means like resonating onomatopoeia in the combination of flitter-and flutter,-for the flute-and flicker, and repetition of prefixes (un-) and participles (unfettered, ungloved, uncluttered). We read a poet who has control – to do what he wishes with that control! – over language, who takes language and plies it to meet his myriad thoughts and urges.

Flipping through the pages unable to approach every poem, I want to make reference to "Red." Colors and nature take center stage:

That colour,
that one and only
colour, occupies
centre stage
and takes a bow.
That one colour,
burning hot as fire
up against the curtain
drawn tight
and white as snow.
That one fire, stark
and bright as the flag
on a white-tailed deer,
bounding up and gone
beneath the boughs.
That leap, sharp
as eyes can read
the contrast,
two colours juxtaposed
and real as winter—
the true north strong
and heading for the trees.

We might think the author is obsessed with colors and vistas yet Di Nardo stands as another worthy heir of the glorious line of poets who are mesmerized by the beauty of what surrounds them. I have said before that "Di Nardo, like most Canadian poets, I can tell, captures the outside sometimes unnoticed world in his poetry." (Taken from my book *In a Fragile Moment. A Landscape of Canadian Poetry*. Hidden Brook Press. 2020)

He dedicates the poem to a poet friend, Tai (Richard Marvin Grove), who is also a painter and photographer. Both poets do know what Di Nardo is describing, they have the insight and the sentience to value such scenes and be transfixed in their beauty.

The reader will feel the limitless vastness limned with a poetic brush, and a sense of motion worded in the highly expressive lines "and takes a bow. / burning hot as fire bright as the flag / on a white-tailed deer, /

bounding up and gone / beneath the boughs / That leap / heading for the trees." This is a *Purdian* poem (another classic being honored?), if you will.

Within the nature-oriented poetry we read in Di Nardo, there are pieces that criticize whatever stands in the way between its beauty and the remote possibility of it being affected, destroyed, defiled. "Home on the Range" is a heartfelt example:

> *Arrows and frigates*
> *Nuclear missiles, F-18s*
> *IEDs and submarines*
> *Bullets and muskets*
> *Daggers and drones*
> *Rifles and pot-shots*
> *Any killing machine—*
> *These are the least*
> *Of my favorite things*
> *When the sky*
> *Is all cloudy and grey*

Skilfully using more expressive means, Di Nardo handles repetition and polysyndeton (the use of *and* in a continuous string of sentences, and hardly any punctuation in the enumeration, which is another expressive means) to make readers shake at the image he builds for them. Therefore, these tools of language become powerful weapons (no pun intended). In the end, the reinforced idea that a sky is not to be "all cloudy and grey" not because of expected rain but because of the warfare airs ("any killing machine") mentioned in the poem.

I have said about Di Nardo that he is "A poet who lives fully and action-immersed, whose feelings and sensations bubble in and around him, explodes in and explores sentiments we humans cannot avoid… Above all, he embarks on a righteous journey of singing to life." (Taken from my book *A Shower of Warm Light. Reviews and Essays on Canadian Poetry*. QuodSermo Publishing. 2021)

Many senses are brought to the paintings this poet offers. These senses are activated through the endless capacity he has to take words and either forcibly hammer them into images or gently sculpt them. Both process and result will always be good given Di Nardo´s gift to pour out what came to him from the outside world but was firstly treated and molded inside his creative mind.

Allow me to close my words on Di Nardo with a poem we wrote in cooperation. It shows the Di Nardo we have always read in his books, it gives us a committed poet whose dynamic mind takes syntax and structure to the next level and alert eyes capture reality and paint it with outstanding word-brushes:

> **this image**
> *In collaboration with Antony Di Nardo*
> *… the divinity of blue. Richard Grove*
>
> cotton shapes
> an azure mantle, this accord
> of white and blue:
>
> under infinity antennas sigh and aim at
> perfect heights
>
> this image
>
> holds a pen
> unfolds a sheet, perpetuates
>
> words

Read then Di Nardo´s book of fine poetry. You will be surprised looking out the window from his words.

Towards Hope
with Mike Madill´s Poetry Book

The Better Part of Some Time
Honourable Mention 2021

"… because there is hope". Job 11:18. The Holy Bible

2021 Don Gutteridge Poetry Award Winner, Mike Madill, holds our hand with a firm grip and ushers us into his *The Better Part of Some Time*, a 2022 Wet Ink Books publication. With an impressive opening piece, "Tether", three sections and fifty-nine poems, Madill is master of theme and readers´ guide along memory lane. Poetry becomes an awesome feat when it successfully limns reality and bleeds motifs no one can avoid relating to. Madill´s writing validates such truth.

"Tether" stands as a formidable overture. The lines (fragments)

> *Every blink a freeze-frame,*
> *tethering befores and afters.*
> *An endless rope-ladder*
> *flung into the unknown.*
>
> *Cling to the belief*
> *of safety in numbers,*
> *like shoaling fish or*
> *flocking birds.*
> *Keep each other in sight,*
> *cherish that tenuous grasp*
> *amidst the tidal drift*
> *of everything unnamed*

invite—exhort, for the poet knows firsthand what *the unknown* has in store, what that *everything unnamed* is. Madill sweats and sheds tears with every single word, every single feeling wrapped in touching remembrances. As Barry Dempster comments: "Madill's poems are clean and thorough; he writes with a chisel on hard rock, sparks flying madly around the room…"

Steve Madill, Mike´s brother and a novelist, says, "Front and centre is the universal experience of the decline and passing of a parent." The hefty notion of loss marks the book and marks *me*, deeply: I lost my father in sad yet unavoidable circumstances and have been writing poems to him ever since. Reading it now, a year after my father passed away, has made me relive moments Madill masterly describes in what Elizabeth Greene deems "A memorable book, impeccably written."

The poet moves across a turbulence of sundry emotions, strong, profound, caustic, reminiscent, hopeful – necessary and unavoidable, because we are human after all – but we see, and welcome, the understandably harrowing shift from grief and helplessness to the courage he musters to survive.

English professor Dr. Linda Burkhardt puts it this way: "Mike Madill's debut collection of poetry traverses the experiences and emotions that make us human, fragile, and humane: childhood wonder and joy, uncertainty, self-doubt, loss, love, friendship, grief, and ultimately the unrelenting hope that keeps us all moving forward."

So, initially we are witness to a poet urged by childhood recollections, haunted by pain, experienced and ingrained in the flesh and the mind, but saved by hope he clings to as we progress through the book. His piece "Personal Effects" (Bedside – 1), for example, is vividly illustrative of the pain (fragments)

> *Two nurses grimly lift the hem of your*
> *blue bed sheet, denying my view of the*
> *doctor removing your intubation tube.*
> *Then, I see your chapped lips, slightly parted,*
> *poised with an unfinished thought... //*

> *... a corner of your blanket dragged*
> *off the bed, draped over your shoulder.*
> *This bloody cornea is like a rage*
> *you'd never shown before,*
> *dashing our final superhero hopes.*
> *Without the breathing tube, he might last*
> *five minutes, an hour at most.*
> *Your chest rises and falls in an almost*
> *imperceptible way... //*
>
> *... Your warm hand,*
> *your grip less than I need. The grit of*
> *pain held so close for so long... //*
> *I stare at your chest, willing it to rise*
> *just once more.*

Later, his poem "Escape Hatch" gives us a readapting, acknowledging, struggling, nostalgic, transformative and perhaps already accepting man (fragments)

> *... counting and*
> *recounting the sides of*
> *my pencil, imagining it*
> *drawing a cartoon escape hatch*
> *on the board room wall.*
>
> *And now here I am, wishing I was*
> *clean and dry and planted behind*
> *a desk again, contorting brain instead*
> *of body. Maybe it's the cat in me*
> *wanting in, then wanting out, in and out,*
> *waffling between worlds.*

Further on in the book, we read his poem "You Are Happy", which flashes that signature Dempster says Madill´s poetry carries: poems "imbued with an honesty that is often stunning" or Dr. Burkhardt says is ever-present: "Amid the existential struggle, though, there emerges a refreshing wit that is often dark but also hopeful. It is a wit that reminds us to laugh at the absurdities of existence…" The poem (full):

> *Remember when you used to wear a watch?*
> *Before you strapped 10,000 steps to your wrist*
> *and your pocket started chirping with texts.*
>
> *Before bark began to peel from the lofty*
> *crimson-king centerpiece in your front yard,*
> *and rust appeared around your vanity's drain.*
>
> *Never mind. Straight back to the dealer —*
> *there's another smudge on your*
> *limited edition Lexus and its opalescent finish.*
>
> *Upgrade your windows before the neighbours notice*
> *they're lowly crank-outs, not double-hung and*
> *triple-glazed. Get that cedar mulch*
> *absurdly mounded around every honey locust*
>
> *because Better Homes and Gardens said so.*
> *Purchase only artisanal potato chips — twice the price,*
> *gluten-free, and everyone will be impressed.*
>
> *Maybe even you. A persona only fully realized*
> *with the walk-in closet you had to wait until*
> *you were forty to find and fill. Now picture yourself*
> *robbed of all the brand names and prestige:*
>
> *no more nine-foot ceilings, three-car garage,*
> *grand piano, in-ground pool. What's left?*
> *Nothing more than me. Ch-ching.*

However mixed we may find the emotions/themes crisscrossing Madill´s book, there remains a bonding aspect to his poems as a solid whole: the acceptance of our human condition, which sees us born, undergo life´s ups and downs (sideway lapses as well), wrinkle into old age and eventually depart. In between are all the involvements and mementoes we build or are thrown into—and hope.

Lisa Burkhardt tells us: "With all of the growing pains, life experiences, joys and loss that make us who we are, Madill takes us there with melancholy ('Alive'), vulnerability ('Smother') and humour ('Ars Poetica'). Enjoy the journey – I know I did."

Able to fathom, capture and *chisel on the hard rock* of writing memories as they emerged, grew, registered and affected his life, Madill soldiers on with a style all his own, plying syntax and word *like they were Byron's or Blake's* to deliver this Don Gutteridge Award winner, that at the end of the day looks at hope prompting us, as Dr. Burkhardt states, "to embrace 'the better part of some time'", because what makes us go on is honoring what's lost, resurfacing after having hit rock bottom, enduring, learning, living and *hoping*.

I have made it almost a habit to include at the end poems of mine related to the themes I review. Wet Ink Books publisher – and generous friend – Richard Grove (Tai) continues to please me by allowing my "whim". I wrote the piece I finish my review with less than two months before my father died. He didn´t have the chance to read the Spanish version… May it serve as a tribute to him and to Madill´s father. Thank you, Tai. Thank you, Mike.

Memories
(To my 84-year-old father, for Father´s Day, June 20th, 2021)
Honor thy father. Deuteronomy 5:16

It hurts to see your spirit cave in
under the burden of Time, unforgiving years
collecting on your shoulders like blankets of age,
heavily cold, coldly heavy. It was me, long ago, on those
shoulders. I remember. I was a merry jockey up there,
my rein your thinning hair or your ears,
me barefoot with my make-believe spurs prodding your chest
so you´d carry me around, so you´d take your
fond-of-horses son out to the street to rival coaches.
I remember. Now, I carry you. Less jollity, more pain

lancing down your legs. *I'm far too old*, you complain,
looking me in the eye as if asking for an explanation.
I cringe at the inevitability of tomorrow—or yesterday,
when eternity stole Mom away. I remember.
Can hardly walk, you mumble. The joyous trots of past days
have cantered down to an effortful walker-assisted shuffle
trying to beat the distance between your bed
and the nearby rocking chair that seems to be, in your mind,
a million miles away. You used to bike to and
from work. I remember. You used to race fishes
in the beach, run athlete-like, carry Mom in your arms…
Today, those memories vanish for you but not for me:
I was there with you, you guided me, you prompted me,
you taught me. I rekindle those stories, retell them
to cheer you up. You say *Thank you*, faintly giving me
a smile of gratitude I'll always remember.

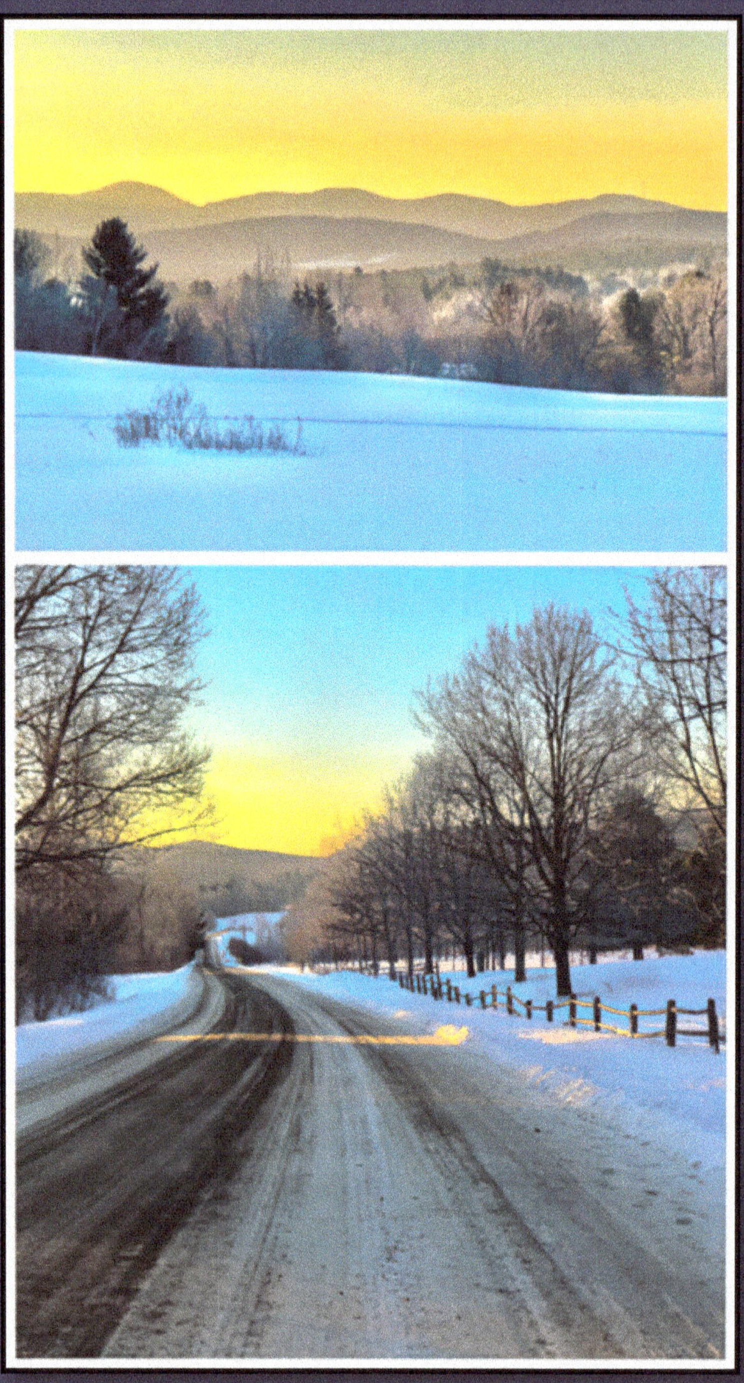

Ann Di Nardo

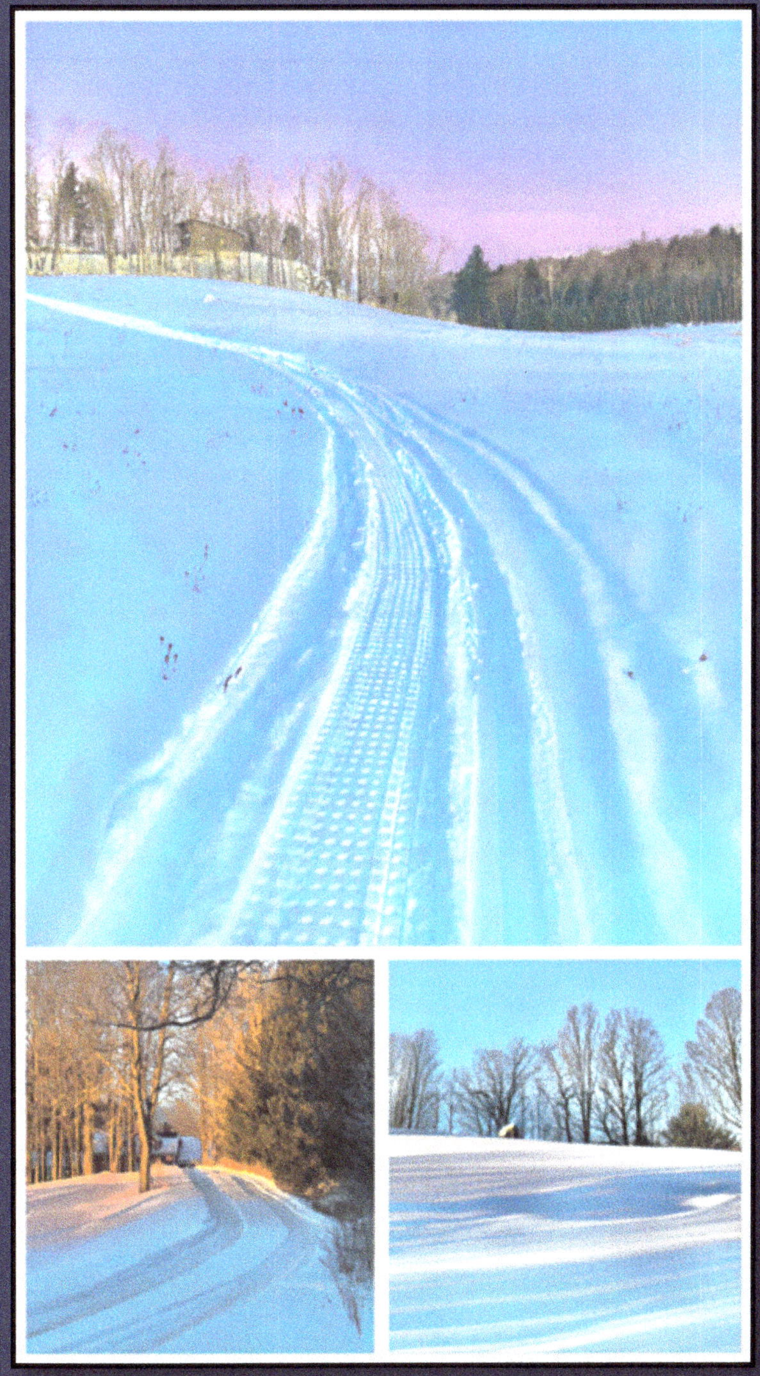

Ann Di Nardo

Sunset Over Walmart

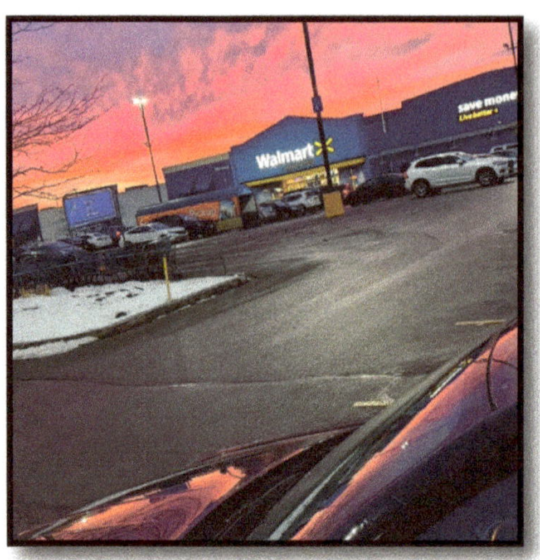

Dear Devour Readers:

Even if you are not listed with Face Book you can still link to this page. Because this FB post is marked "Public" anyone can link in at: https://www.facebook.com/richard.grove.9678. Take a look at the Sunset Over Walmart poems and post your poem. The posting is a little bit down, at December 28, 2022 - you will see the Walmart sunset pic.

My dear wife Kim and I stopped at the Cobourg Walmart just after Christmass, 2022. The sun was setting. This is the pic I took with my phone. An hour later I wrote this below poem and posted it on FaceBook with the invitation for anyone else to write and post their own Sunset Over Walmart poem.

The following poems are the results. They are not in any particular order other than mostly in the oder that they arrive.

You are invited to post your own poem.

all the best

tai

Richard M. Grove / Tai
Sunset Over Walmart

Does the sun ever set
over the neon moon
of mass marketing
China imports
that have become
the ubiquitous symbol of
need and want?
The juxtaposition of
insatiable hunger confuses
emotional starvation with
must-have-needs.
More,
more,
more,
bigger,
better,
faster,
bluer,
greener,
sexier,
sweeter.
My body,
my mind,
my soul
all want the sun
to never set
over Walmart.

John B. Lee

Sunset Over Walmart

somewhere
in the crimson overcast
of the heavens of Cobourg
blazing over the monochromatic mall
called Walmart
there dwells an angel
wielding a sword of warning
forged in the mind of Milton
walking the light
over the hardpacked Eden
of the parking lot
as hand in hand he and Dante Alighieri
scribing a lovelorn lamentation
for the lost sheepfold
on the wall above the gate
this drab-souled graffito
a singular augury
for chrome-cart commerce
is all that remains
of the ancient agora
here where little baskets of Peruvian blueberries
await the wine-maker's gaze
and good mothers
with money enough
for a second glance
at the dry cellars of ancient Rome
look to where the greengrocer fades
into the earth like dust in the spade of the tell
and someone inquires of a future archeologist
"what time is it?"
and he answers "now, and then"

Don Gutteridge

Sunset Over Walmart
Walmart A-Lot

There is something surreal
about the Walmart, perched
on the late-day pavement,
the letters of its calling-card,
a bloated alabaster alphabet
touting iss timely merchandizing
arrival to anyone friendless
enough to be caught walking
this arid lot for autos
and restless pedestrians,
but wait, look up and gaze
amazed at the sunset sky
above the clutter of cars,
where a crimson mist is adrift
on its own motionless ocean
of air, and whatever we do
with our brick-and-mortar schemes,
there will always be beauty –
to startle, and heal.

Antony Di Nardo

Sunset Over Walmart
Walmart Specials

1

Sunsets, sunrise, dawn or dusk
Can be had for pennies less
If you park at Walmart and ask
For the customer loyalty discount
Pack that has you coming back
For more and more each time
The sky lights up and leaves you
Dumbfounded, and in the red

2

Nobody paints the sky quite like
Masters of the Universe, Wall
Street types who create value
By adding zeroes, or the Walmart
Neon that drains the sky of colour

3

For one day only—the Sunset Special—
Stick around till closing time,
Fill your cart up to the brim,
And for the low price of your soul
We'll throw in the moon and the stars.
Next week, the Northern Lights!

Ronda Wicks Eller

Sunset Over Walmart

brilliant hues
red and pink
shades of Canadian
funny money $50
bills i wish were in my wallet
hunkered down
in the sunset
over Walmart
i would spend those babies
frivolously
then and there
if only
i wasn't standing
on the outside
looking in and
contemplating
the sunset
heralding
an unravelling night
the episodic symbolism
of a coming cheap seat
shopping
dream

Bruce Kauffman
sunset over **Walmart**

it is never this obstacle
in the foreground
it is earth's
          ever-sky behind

i am lost in these colours
twilight   this sunset

these pinks and maroons
this lavender
burgundy wisps rolling

ever changing
          these colours of dusk
i want to lose myself in it

to now jump off the top
of this inconvenient building
before me
i will leap   become air-borne
will soar   above all else
          at 1670 kilometres per hour

i will travel   joyfully
inside this evolving colour
forever

i will never return

Richard-Yves Sitoski
Sunset Over Walmart

from the parking lot
the Walmart is a lantern
immense and lurid

inside the smell
of stripper and wax
from last night's renewals

if an odour
could be plangent
this would be

vegetables looking wrong
too perfect round and red
the green an intrusion of summer

sweatshop clothing
free from cruelty-free
the price for low prices

things will not be different
once you are asleep
till then you tread

the glossy floor
with exaggerated caution
thinking every step

will make a splash
you are confounded
by the dryness.

K.V. Skene

Sunset Over Walmart

It is a truth universally acknowledged
that sumptuous sunsets over Walmart
endanger the brain and overexposure
to big-box stores
lingers long after you've lumbered home
overburdened and broke – massive
monumentalism,
superfluous selectivity
plus stupefied sensibilities
can lead to fatalities
and/or long-term depression/obsession
with gigantism. Big
is bad for your mental health – but
small (believe it or not)
is also beautiful.

Mike Madill
Sunset Over Walmart

The evening's sky is inflamed
above this hangar-sized store,
just another link in a teeming

chain of discounted fare
and best-you-can-do wares,
swollen blue shiner

for a town that never heals.
'Made in Canada' simply isn't
in the budget anymore, honey.

Once prices that can't be beat
fail to siphon free all the crimson
from another month's bottom line,

you might finally give in, try on
the sloppy vest and nametag,
price-match QR codes presented

on trophy wives' sparkly iPhones,
pretend to check the fine print
on clipped and wrinkled coupons

offered up by the shaking hands
of old dears. Pulling little more
than minimum wage behind

the till just so you can watch
another meal of Pizza-Pop
leftovers slowly spin

in the dim light of your
microwave, or maybe splurge
for a quarter-pounder

with cheese, wondering
if you can still afford
to get fries with that.

Shane Joseph
Sunset Over Walmart

The sun may not set on the Walmart Empire,
Like it did on the British,
Much to old Churchill's dismay.
I do not shop at the Walmart Empire
I don't dig "more, more, more."
Thus my finances are not in disarray.

Susan Brannigan-Rampp
Sunset Over Walmart

She ditched her AA meeting tonight
Nestling in Johnny Walker's cocoon
Not even noticing I stayed out all night
Sleeping in the Walmart parking lot
Next to the retirees' winnebago
In the shopping cart
Return tent

Wendy Maclean
Sunset Over Walmart

alerts the sky.
No big specials today, only plastic
promises and cheap knocked off dreams.
Clouds offer consolation.
Beauty can never be bought or sold.
Love is always the best special
and it is priceless.

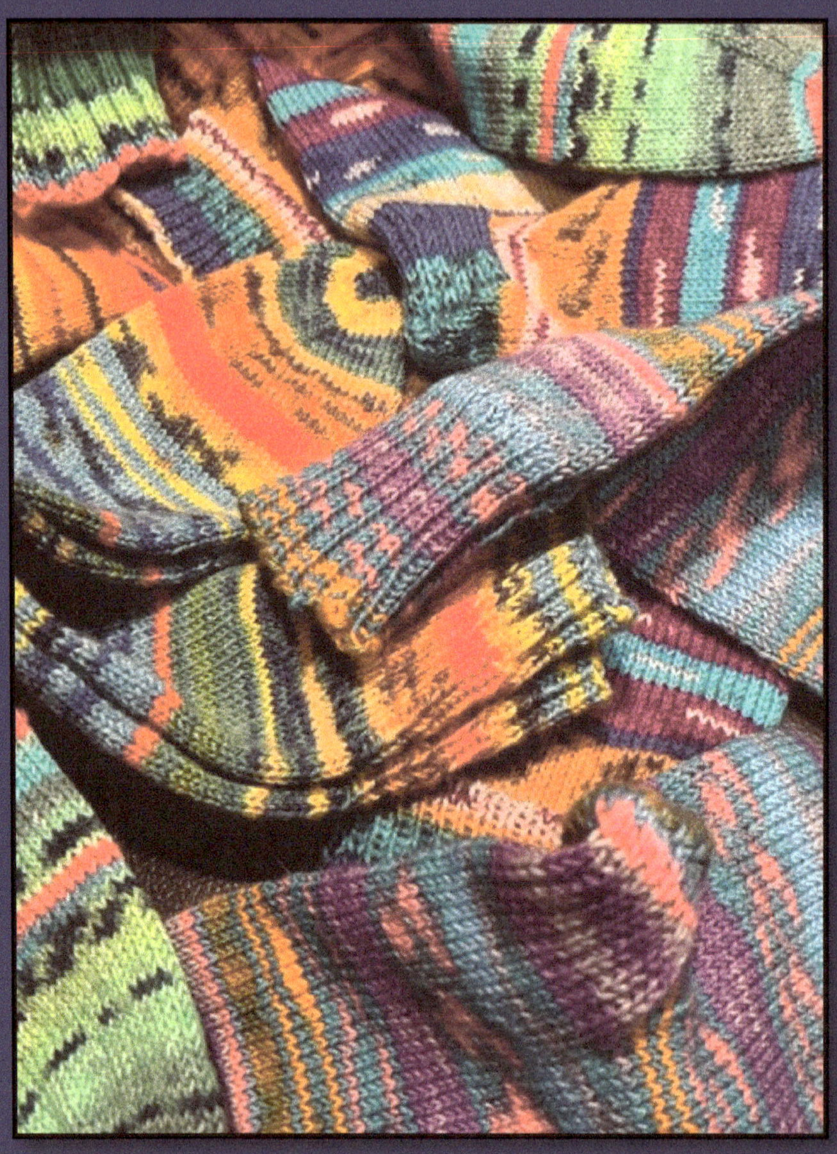

Ann Di Nardo

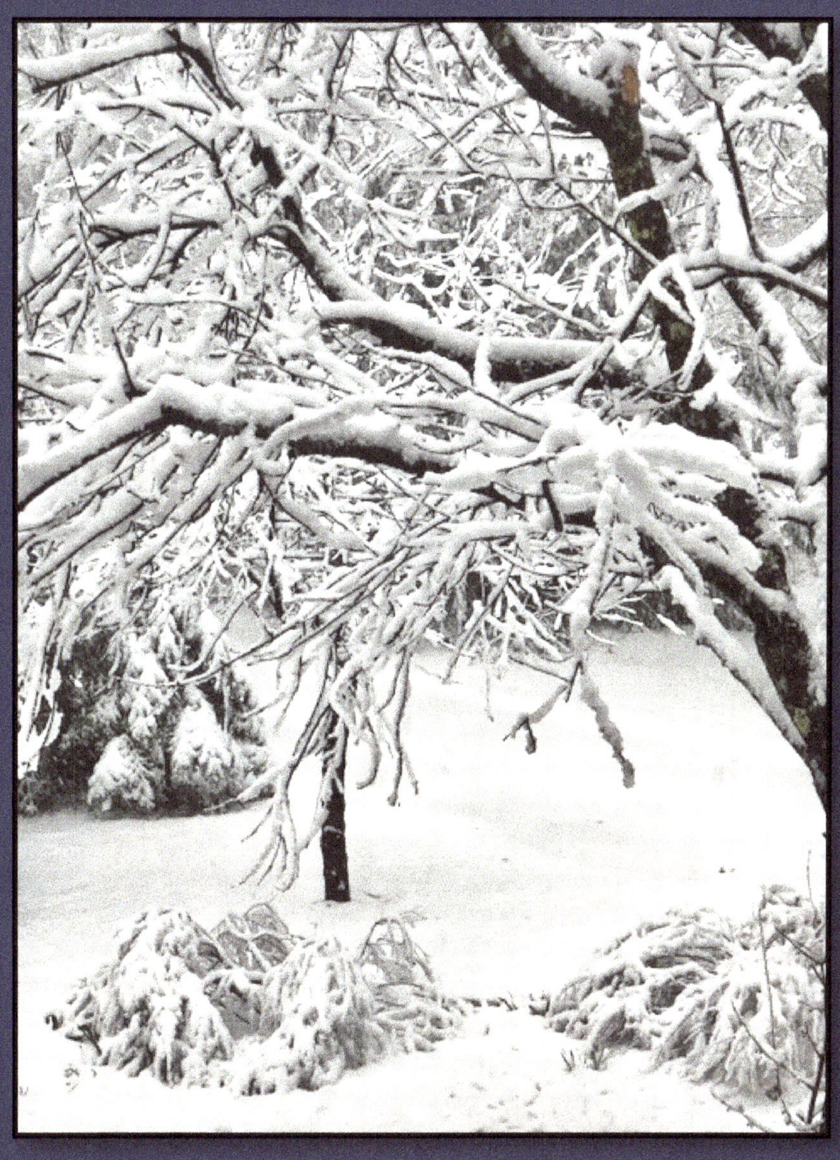

Ann Di Nardo

Wet Ink Books

www.ingramcontent.com/pod-product-compliance
Lightning Source LLC
Chambersburg PA
CBHW050032040726
47599CB00015B/1640